Six Steps
to Creating Profit

A GUIDE FOR SMALL AND MID-SIZED
SERVICE-BASED BUSINESSES

Patricia Sigmon

WILEY

John Wiley & Sons, Inc.

Published by John Wiley & Sons, Inc., Hoboken, New Jersey.
Published simultaneously in Canada.

For general information on our other products and services or for technical support,
please contact our Customer Care Department within the United States at (800)
762-2974, outside the United States at (317) 572-3993 or fax (317) 572-4002.

Wiley also publishes its books in a variety of electronic formats. Some content that
appears in print may not be available in electronic books. For more information about
Wiley products, visit our web site at www.wiley.com.

Library of Congress Cataloging-in-Publication Data:

Sigmon, Patricia, 1950–
   Six steps to creating profit : a guide for small and mid-sized service-based
businesses / Patricia Sigmon.
      p. cm.
   Includes index.
   ISBN 978-0-470-55425-8 (cloth)
   1. Profit.   2. Service industries.   3. Small business.   I. Title.
   HB601.S555 2010
   658.15′54–dc22

                                                            2009046289

Printed in the United States of America

10 9 8 7 6 5 4 3 2 1

to my mother, Patricia Velten, who shared her entrepreneurial spirit with her five daughters,

to my husband, Lyle, who helped me to have a great time, and

to my three greatest accomplishments in life: my children, Christie, Robin, and David.

Contents

Contents

Contents

Contents

Foreword

Years ago I was on my first e-commerce deal and I was hesitant to charge enough to make a profit. "A guy like that can handle a number like $50,000 because he needs the solution," Patricia Sigmon leaned over and whispered to me in the plush boardroom. And with that prompt, I bumped my price, asked for the business, and won a profitable project for my new consulting company.

That was a memorable day for me. Patricia's advice was so simple and clear. It made all the difference. And now, Patricia shares her secrets for making your business more profitable in *Six Steps to Creating Profit*. These hard-won tips are here for the taking.

I found my head nodding as I turned each page. Many of the tips are common sense. Some are surprising. Time and time again Patricia reminds us that we—the owners—are the driving force behind our businesses. We need to create positive change. That is the one constant in business and in life.

Patricia points out that profit makes your business strong. Profit makes it possible for you to meet your obligations. Profit gives you options. *Six Steps to Creating Profit* details the continuous process that you need to check prices, reevaluate old ways, and take advantage of new tools; and in today's Internet world, continually adjusting to fast-changing forces is more necessary than ever.

The lessons here are as important to experienced business owners as they are to those of you just starting out. Even I learned new things I need to do for my business.

The book concludes with what I believe to be its strongest point: You must make everyone in your company a salesperson. Gone are the days when only the owner or lone salesperson was responsible for generating revenue. Enrolling all employees in the sales process throws a wider net to generate more profit. It turns your team members into solutions providers and profit makers.

Six Steps to Creating Profit is filled with pertinent lists. I return to Patricia's lists of key questions again and again. Each time I consider the questions, I see a fresh new perspective. How can I apply this now? How can I solve a customer's problem? What forces are changing the business landscape? How can my business remain relevant? This book reminds us how important the processes of constant improvement and problem solving truly are.

I am fond of saying "Problems are our friends." I feel they encourage us to improve the way we assess, respond, create, plan, implement, and lead. You should always be willing to think, question, recommend, and review. *Six Steps to Creating Profit* provides a framework for positive change leading you to more profit.

Let this be *your* memorable day—the day you take on the *Six Steps to Creating Profit*.

David R. Harris
President, EC Internet

Preface

Starting a business and staying in business is not an easy task. And, as if having business longevity isn't enough of an accomplishment, the business is expected actually to make a good profit. Profits help the owner to get paid, help to fund retirement accounts, help to fund college accounts, help create good business valuations to attract future buyers, help with cash flow, help with bonuses, and help create a safety net should something go wrong.

Most business books that are on the market address the "normal" processes of a business—How to Start a Business; How to Write a Business Plan; How to Be a Great Salesperson; How to Develop a Marketing Plan; How to Be a Project Manager. Everything you need to know to set up shop, get a client, and service the client is available in many a How-To guide.

But what about the daily trials and tribulations of cash flow, missing profits, shrinking sales, new competition, or a stale workforce? What about the business model where sales are devoured by expenses? Or the model where you are working more and making less? How can sales be increased, business expanded, longevity attained, and profits realized when the daily grind of money, collections, and lack of profits continues to take center stage? If there is a broken business model, there are ways to get it fixed!

Certainly, not all businesses are alike. Yet, among privately-held, service-based, small to mid-sized businesses, there are a lot of similarities. There is an owner, a founder, a president, a boss—someone who calls the shots, makes the big decisions, and takes the big falls. There is labor being performed—service to clients. It could be legal, accounting, consulting, office cleaning, painting, plumbing, nursing, or any number of other services. The business feels the strains of the economy, cash flow, or missing profits almost immediately and often needs to mingle personal and business matters and money.

For these businesses, there are six tried and true steps that deal with the everyday problems that, ultimately, show themselves very clearly in one place—lack of profit. In each of these steps, there are several examples where renovation and reengineering of old practices will result in a more streamlined, profitable business model, centered on profitable sales.

In this book, the following six steps are explored along with suggested changes to the business model:

Chapter 1: Changing the Rules of Operation. New sales centers, expense-cutting suggestions, computerized profit and loss, labor utilization, and sales tracking are discussed.

Chapter 2: Staying Visible and Connected. Marketing-geared credentials and Internet-based strategic alliance programs are explored with sales generation in mind.

Chapter 3: Maximizing Cash Flow. Cash-flow-friendly sales models, income and expense budgets, and managing up-to-the minute profit and loss numbers are detailed.

Chapter 4: Streamlining Management Costs. Streamlining administration, creating new profit centers, and maintaining up-to-date, synchronized, shareable company data are discussed.

Chapter 5: Raising the Marketing Bar. New Internet marketing methods, updated standard marketing methods, and return on investment computerized measurement are explored.

Chapter 6: Making Everyone a Salesperson. Replacement of an expense-geared business model with a sales-geared, marketing-driven, data-rich business model is presented.

A company looking to solve profit problems may be a new company starting out, trying to learn from other's mistakes and avoid profit pitfalls. Or it might be a highly successful, already profitable business looking for new profit-making ideas. But the companies most needing help are the ones that are just barely getting by with their profit model or the ones deep in red ink with a model that may close the business doors very soon.

There is no comparison between a new business and an old business as far as life experience goes. So, cures for profit problems in a long-standing model cannot be oversimplified. Complex problems call for complex solutions.

In Appendix A, "The How-To Guide to Creating Profit" and Appendix B, "Scheduling the Changes" you will be able to choose what business changes should be made, schedule those changes, and prepare for ongoing reevaluation in the future.

No matter what, if a company has been around for some time selling a service and pleasing clients, something "right" has been going on. To help boost the bottom line, it's the "wrong" that needs to be found and fixed. This book is about the fix.

Acknowledgments

If I had been in any other business than the computer field for the last 30 years, I probably would not be able to write this book.

The business changes that have taken place since personal computers hit the market in the early 1980s are nothing short of revolutionary.

Where else but in a computer business would you:

- Invest all of your money in something that you knew would be obsolete in a few months
- Train your staff intently knowing they would need retraining shortly or that they would be leaving to take another job soon
- Sell software that didn't work unless the client paid for repairs
- Sell products where a client needed to prepay for a year's worth of "fixes" so the product would still function
- Write programs where you couldn't possibly, as a human, identify and plan for everything that might go wrong

Yes, it has been an interesting few decades and, just like having "no service" on a cell phone has become an accepted form of annoyance, so too have software bugs, viruses, spam, and all of the other pains of computerland become part of a new normal.

The point is that there has been no standard in this field that hasn't been subject to reinvention.

Acknowledgments

So, the challenges of earning a living and making a profit in a service-based business, with the most outrageous, newly-conceived, client-unfriendly business models, make the problems of almost any other line of business seem easy to fix.

For this exact reason, I've been able to shed light on many a business profit problem for clients and peers over the years. For those of us in the computer field who have longevity, we have fought many wars and have been "around the block"—nothing has been sacred.

Learning on the job, reinventing the wheel, selling a solution that was supposed to work but didn't, and training clients who were completely untrainable—without things like prepayment and maintenance contracts, there would be no computer field.

Starting with my first client, Jerry Cohen of Williams Real Estate in New York City, and my first official vendor, Bob Davies of SBT Accounting Systems in California, I thank every person who had more wisdom than I had and who helped me to formulate, under those technically trying circumstances, the most reasonable business model that was possible.

There were other early business mentors who I admired, such as Rod Hatcher of TIW in Pennsylvania, who seemed to be born with a perfectly formulated business plan and David Harris of EC Internet in California, who never heard a technical question that he couldn't answer and never saw a programming language that he didn't want to learn. Jeff Childers, a techie from Florida, consulted with me for an hour at a convention and helped me to set up a billing model which has lasted for a decade and a half and which I have passed on to many a struggling business owner. And, there was Susan Sheridan, an original Microsofter, who moved to the land of marketing and helped all of us computer folk become marketers.

There would have been no business, however, without my husband, Lyle. As a sign of the times, he read every technical book he could find so that he could install the hardware that I didn't want to touch. He cold-called new clients, made me smile even when my programs crashed, and, eventually, threw his accountant's hat away and joined the technical revolution.

Finally, as a computer business owner in the 1990s, the New Jersey Association of Women Business Owners (NJAWBO) set me on the path of spreading the business word, allowing me to volunteer, teach classes, speak at conventions, and mentor new company owners. That has led to the pleasure of working for almost two decades with other business owners, helping them to solve their problems and make a profit. Hence, this book.

Introduction

Despite the difficulties of running a business, many owners of small to mid-sized service-based firms are able to be the masters of their craft, have a long list of repeat clients, and even enjoy a great reputation. What many are missing, however, is a good profit. Where do the CEOs, the founders, the owners of these small to mid-sized firms go to figure out why they are no longer earning what they once earned or, even why their employees are making more money than they are?

Unbelievably, many an entrepreneur will spend an entire business week working to "make payroll" without a single moment's thought about the bottom line.

With credit crunch and cash flow fears looming, structural business changes geared toward beefing up the net profit never seem to make the top ten on any given day's "to-do list."

Does the bottom line profit matter so much? Many a small to mid-sized business owner is a pillar of the community, serving on boards, donating to charity, golfing with clients, partying with employees and their families. What great harm is a little red ink?

Of course, this isn't a reasonable question and every business owner knows why profits matter. It is the owners' duty to protect their businesses so that their families and employees are safe, their retirement and children's college accounts are funded, and at the same time keep a healthy valuation for management for the next generation or attraction of an eventual buyer.

So, if not having respectable profits in one's business is the ailment, where do we look to find the cure? What are the roadblocks that prevent a business from solving its profit problems? Who exactly is in need of help here? And, finally, in a nutshell, how do we fix a broken model?

Profit-making advice in the small to mid-sized market is not an easy find. It's far easier to learn "how to make a great sales presentation" or "how to design a website" than it is to find ways to increase the bottom line and drive profits. Business "How-To" books are usually just that: books on how to do the business at hand. Profit 101 tactics are squeezed between the lines but Profit 201 tactics are rarely spelled out—sophisticated lessons in being lean and mean, making the hard decisions, and raising profitability to Mission Statement level.

And as if finding profit-cures isn't hard enough, the real roadblocks to making change in a privately held small to mid-sized business usually rest in the hands of the owners themselves. After all, who are these owners, these founders, these CEOs? How did they get where they are?

They are entrepreneurs, risk takers, "bosses" who have staked their claim on a certain niche and are proud of their accomplishments. Sometimes the whole family is employed at one of these firms. Every client knows the owner's name and deals with this company for (sometimes) personal reasons.

Technology, however, more than any other factor, has invaded the space of the traditional small to mid-sized service business—buying online, selling online, real time questions, real time answers. The rules of the game have changed—and they have changed quickly.

Seasoned business owners will remember their first computer, the day they first "faxed," and the day they bought their first "car" phone. However, now, the speed of change necessitates radically modifying not only business tools in place but new purchasing methods, employee behaviors, competitive pricing, and visibility in the marketplace. And that's just the beginning.

If a company has profit problems even when armed with the most up-to-date tools, then the time-honored business culture that made the company what it is today probably needs adjusting. The owner who has nurtured a firm like a beloved child may be reluctant to see the writing on the wall, or can see the writing but may stubbornly refuse to take a step backward and make the changes that need to be made.

If starting a business once brought out creative juices, changing a business model to meet the demands of a new marketplace—resulting in a more profitable structure—can be exhilarating. But, the boss needs to get on board!

So, what is the profile of a company that needs help in the profit area?

For a new business about to be started, it can be advantageous for a founder to read about profit pitfalls, and try to catch the problem before it begins.

But which business owners who are out there already need to revamp their profit-making formulas?

First of all, an owner with a profitable business may want to stay ahead of the pack, find new profit areas, look for new trends, and stay as lean as can be, maximizing net income wherever possible. Even a company with a healthy bottom line needs to address change constantly, cater to a younger, more technological workforce, and compete with a global, ever-reinventing marketplace.

Another owner owns a long-term business where the model hasn't changed very much over the years but the net profit has—in a downward fashion. This owner may have respectable gross sales but, looking toward retirement, sees a business with diminishing profits, longer work hours for the owner, and a valuation that is not attractive to an investor now, and won't be when the need arises. This owner has a valuable list of clients and can perform a great service, but manages a model where all income is absorbed by expenses. This owner has a great deal to gain by implementing some changes that will affect the bottom line.

Maybe another owner isn't so close to retirement but, rather, needs to look at 20 or 30 more years in the workplace. There have been clients; there has been profit but the business is shaky. Whether it can withstand the forces of the economy is questionable, but everything that can be done should be done before giving up the entrepreneurial dream. A lot of work is done by this owner to try to keep clients happy; many times the work is done for free. There's also a lot of hope here in the future—the big jobs that will come from investing now in client relationships; the passionate "hobby" part of the business where a great deal of work is done without any income, purely for pleasure.

Finally, there is the "what am I going to do" business owner. The doors are open but may be closing fast due to dire circumstances. Is there anything to salvage here? There might be. Any service business with a list of clients, a service that meets a need, and an owner with an open ear may find avenues to explore that were previously unknown, or did not even exist in the past.

So, we know we are looking for a better bottom line (either out of necessity or intellectual curiosity). We know it's hard to find sophisticated advice regarding profit generation but, when it is found, we need to overcome any inappropriate owner resistance to effecting necessary change. And, when all is said and done, no matter what fixes, changes, or enhancements are added to the business culture, pure and simple, net income has to be put in the forefront of the business model. Profit making needs to be a leading factor in every business decision. It needs to be an everyday, real-time effort and not a once-a-year event discussed with the CPA. Just as cash flow and payroll requirements hold steady visibility, profit fever needs to stay in the limelight. Every sale, every paycheck, and every purchase has to be measured with company net profit in mind. Each employee, also, needs to be put on the profit bandwagon, not the expense bandwagon. Processes and methods that are broken need to be fixed and they need to stay fixed. And, this reinvention needs to be ongoing. Twenty-first-century small to mid-sized businesses are fluid, ever-changing models that can't afford to remain static.

Looking at business models that seem, at first glance, to have more differences with your business than similarities might seem like a big waste of time. It can, however, provide just the change of pace and insight into new thinking that you are looking for. After all, you probably know a lot about your direct competitors, and, have long ago addressed missing components in your comparable sales model. But looking at a "business to consumer" company can help a "business to business" company reengineer itself, and understanding a manufacturing model can help your service company.

However your business began, you borrowed ideas, knew what companies you wanted to emulate and which ones you didn't, eventually settling on your own individual image.

Profit-making ideas can be borrowed from all walks of business life. Hearing new thoughts, taking a closer look at a model that you previously ignored and, in general, opening your eyes to new business thinking will go a long way to solving your profit problems that have crept up over the years.

So, looking for a better profit is all about change—not changing the best parts that a company has grown to offer, but filling in the weak spots.

The business, change and all, needs to continue to perform a great service, satisfy customers, and keep employees happy, but most importantly, this has to be done while making a good profit.

1

Changing the Rules
of Operation

Goals

- Increase sales
- Decrease expenses
- Streamline administration

Increasing Sales

At one time, the business in question had all of the right formulas for sales and profit, but today things are slipping. There is competition everywhere and the bottom line is thinner and thinner. This chapter offers a fresh look at some ways to take yesterday's successful model and tune it up for the next decade.

Cross-Selling

Cross-selling is all about selling more goods and services to your existing clients. There are certainly plenty of examples of bad and inappropriate cross-selling, but for a busy consumer one-stop shopping is more appreciated than ever. Being a full-service firm and offering complementary services or product offerings can keep a staff at maximum operating levels and at the same time keep happy customers out of the competitor's hands.

It is not that cross-selling is a new phenomenon. It just needs a fresh ongoing look in a seasoned business model.

In the old days, for instance, a software consulting company would sell preprinted forms to its customer base. Every business computer system needed invoices, checks, and other kinds of forms. Then laser printers arrived and the forms all but disappeared. Now this same software company doesn't sell preprinted forms, but it might sell website hosting or email hosting services to its clients.

Just looking at the state of today's telephone companies illustrates this. It used to be enough of a convenience to be able to buy a telephone when you signed up for your new phone number. Now, you can order high speed Internet, wireless access, and even cable television along with your phone service—all from one vendor, all offered by one salesperson, and all on one monthly bill.

Similarly, when your accounting firm does their audit, selling an in-house financial system, bookkeeping data-entry assistance, or even document-imaging services for your crowded files may be up for discussion. And, visiting your bank's branch manager may result in credit line, charge card, and financial management applications.

Does your chiropractor also sell the services of a nutritionist? Are vitamins available? Massage therapy? Personal training sessions?

And what about the veterinarian who sells pet food, provides grooming, boarding, and even counseling?

The trick is to complement your main offering, utilizing the value of your client base and the value of your productive operation.

When you can't imagine what you can add to your sales repertoire and can't think of how you can add more value to the relationship you have with your clientele, just look at your own personal purchases and service needs. Does your lawn care provider also clean your gutters and shovel your snow? Doesn't this make you happy? What would be an effective additional offering to add to your service mix? Clients are busy; if they have found a satisfying relationship, they are more than happy to avoid searching for other service providers for the many complementary add-on offerings that surround the services you provide. And, searching online for your competitors' cross-selling concepts will open your eyes to many new opportunities envisioned by others.

Relationship Selling

When business is drying up, it is hard to imagine where the clients have gone. They probably just don't need your service right now but, sadly, when they do need your service, you have to do more than hope that they remember you. Certain fields lend themselves to problem-only communications—plumbing, pest control, hardware repair shops, and other reactive-type businesses. Taking a lead from more proactive business models, the goal here is to sell a relationship and not a one-time solution.

When you visit the personal trainer at the gym, a series of ten or twenty visits will be offered; computer consultants will present retainer plans covering 50 or 100 labor hours. Additionally, if you want your furnace or your air conditioner serviced on a weekend, hopefully, you will have signed up, in advance, for a monthly service plan. All sorts of yearly start-up plans, preventive maintenance plans, and discounted repair plans have become commonplace in certain fields.

So, why not in your field? Just because you haven't operated this way in the past does not mean you can't change course. Many a business's doors would not be open if a steady dose of relationship selling wasn't taking place. It's all about continuity!

There are certainly customers who won't want an ongoing relationship. For these "tough sells" it behooves the business owner to relate to the true benefits that can be served to the customer and then "make an offer that can't be refused" rather than provide a one-time-only service.

Inexpensive monthly maintenance plans, for example, keep you in contact with your clients, if not in person, at least on a monthly invoice.

And, by all means, we aren't looking to fool a client into repeat credit card charges for something like unwanted credit reports. What we do want is to maintain a mutually beneficial professional relationship with a happy customer. You want to be the first on the list to be called when your brand of expert attention is needed.

Like the yearly chimney cleaning service, the weekly pool cleaning service, or the spring and fall lawn clean up, the trick is to apply relationship-selling techniques to a one-time-only service model.

Vertical versus Horizontal Selling

If you sell your services to the masses, no matter who the masses are, you are probably selling horizontally. You may install alarm systems, sell computer hardware services, or train users on word-processing and spreadsheet programs. You can provide these same services for anyone who calls. In this case, growing your sales volume may be all about growing your vertical markets. By identifying a small subset of your client base, say restaurants, you can repackage your offerings geared to the restaurant industry. If you design websites, you would have a restaurant website design service; an advertising business can develop a PR campaign for restaurants while a decorating firm can specialize in redecorating restaurants. The same holds true for many other "vertical" markets, such as banks or hotels.

The goal is to create a vertical sales offering where you didn't have one before. Your client base can provide a wealth of information on different vertical markets to enter.

For instance, you may already happen to have several packaging companies as your clients. Your next advertising campaign can be to all area packaging companies where your "packaging company solution" will be touted.

And, if you are the personal trainer for several weekend golfers, your "golf regimen" can be a great marketing theme.

It is expensive to create brand-new product offerings, but when you have a successful solution that requires only remarketing, start-up costs are kept down, staff is kept busy, and sales are increased.

Similarly, if you have been dedicating your efforts to vertical markets, it may be time to go after the masses. If you have long been selling to manufacturers, for instance, and this business category is operating at an all-time low, it is time to repackage the offerings you have to attract a wider audience. Instead of your "soup to nuts" financial and inventory service for, say, clothing manufacturers, break the solution apart. You'll find a bigger audience for a pure "financial" solution where you already have the expertise that you need.

The trick is to expand whatever market base you have to keep or create new vertical customer bases while you segregate a section of your business that can serve a more general public.

Expanding Your Market

If you have been servicing $5 million to $200 million businesses for your whole business life and sales are shrinking while profits too are slowly disappearing, then it may be time to look at customers who are bigger or smaller. What can you apply to your $5 million customers that you can also apply, with a little strategy, to a smaller client?

Smaller clients may feed into your preferred mid-sized market in the future; or, better yet, just by marketing to a smaller client, you may lure the new customer into a larger solution than they thought they would need. This new business avenue can sustain your own employee base and open new opportunities for client referrals, cross-selling, relationship sales, and vertical or horizontal sales.

At a time when many laid-off workers are becoming self-employed or when businesses are downsizing or emerging from bankruptcy, changing your model and handling a smaller account than you usually would service may bring in needed revenue and—with operations that are already in-house—at a better profit margin than starting a new line of business would normally generate.

For example, an ad agency may service large, national real estate firms writing press releases and ads that sell multimillion dollar homes in vacation hot spots. There is no start-up investment required if you perform that same service in a more limited fashion for local realtors with lower-priced homes for sale.

No matter what, if a smaller client needs to have a lower price point, then, there has to be a change in deliverables. Repackaging your service could include a 45-minute session instead of a 60-minute session, or a smaller portion of your normal product offering. In any case, expanding into a lower-tiered market can help fill a gap.

The same holds true for bigger clients. For instance, something you do for a $200 million company might also work departmentally in a billion dollar company. Larger corporations have departmental budgets and departmental needs, and, many times, one hand is not washing the other! One large corporation can house several sets of business leads, each comparable to the size of a smaller sized client. Many times, you can be "passed around" from one department to another once you get your foot in a large corporation's door. Transitioning your business to cover larger and smaller markets can keep your staff busy and build your reference base.

The trick here is to think outside of the box. Slightly changing your market may be a quick and effective fix in a downturn and can provide an ongoing lead base for your real market in the future.

Using Loss Leaders

Looking at many other industries, we have become familiar with the "get them in the door" tactics of, say, cell phone service providers or supermarkets. The free phone generates years of monthly fees and the free sugar sits in a filled shopping cart. Similarly, you may receive a free printer when you order your new laptop. Of course, the printer will need plenty of ink cartridges in its lifetime. These uses of loss leaders are well known enough in the retail world, but are there loss leaders that service and professional businesses use? Are there any respectable sounding offers that aren't stamped with the word *gimmick*?

Of course there are, but we need to think hard and see how the use of such a tactic might be beneficial.

If you sit with a business owner at a Rotary Club meeting, you may hear about the office needing painting, the secretary going on medical leave, or the salespeople needing laptops. Relationships are rarely built using direct mail flyers. Especially, in a service business, we need to meet people, work with them, establish credibility, and find common ground for future business. So, when an attorney offers inexpensive wills, an accountant provides low-cost financial aid form prep, or an advertising agency offers a specially priced newspaper ad, these low- or no-profit services can be viewed as loss leaders. Just as the free phone brings the ultimate goal—monthly service fees—when a client has a positive experience, they are more likely to remember all of the other similar services that they may need from your firm.

The trick, of course, is to do the best job that can be done whether the job is hugely profitable or not profitable at all. No one wants to rehire you for doing a poor job just because it didn't carry a big price tag.

Brand Extensions

Although much more common with products than services, well-known brands can offer new items for sale which will immediately have a label known to the customer—the brand name. So, if a new furniture line is introduced by a popular clothing manufacturer, it immediately has the authenticity and marketing power that the original clothing line had established.

Service firms are using this same model to generate an immediate buzz about a new niche that they try to enter: Smith Heating announces Smith Carpentry and Jones Plumbing announces Jones Electrical. There is enough similarity in the two businesses' audience for customers to use the new services without feeling the need to research or compare prices to other vendors. Like cross-selling, the original business model is being enhanced with new items to sell to the same client base. However, the brand extension is bigger than just another list of services. It is usually in a separate product or service category, denoting a much more major investment and expansion by the business.

So, what kind of brand extensions can a service business offer? Well, looking around at businesses that are different than yours can provide all of the answers.

A group of orthopedic doctors create a physical therapy center; an established medical group adds a pharmacy. An accounting firm opens a computer support division. Your building's well-known developer opens a nearby supermarket or a concierge business using the building's famous name. A day care center opens an evening babysitting business with kiddy movies and chicken fingers to boot. Using the brand name, the location, and the client base of your business, opening a new division will generate an automatic draw. And, once the new line is fully operational, business will travel back and forth as the new entity generates its own buzz.

The trick here is to have offerings that are usually done by other companies, capitalizing on the strength of your market share to build immediate interest and more quickly expand.

Replacing Yesterday's Stale Successes with Today's Winners

Every service business performs labor of some kind. Sometimes, products are sold purely to generate labor revenue and sometimes labor is sold in order to sell a product. In any case, the need for the services or products offered may disappear over time.

In only the last 25 years, the Internet has removed the need for phone books, cell phones have replaced reliance on land lines, and ATMs, E-ZPass, and bar coding has replaced many manual processes, creating electronic connectivity never before imagined. Where can an owner go to explore replacing their successful sales solutions of yesteryear? Are there replacements? What have other widget trainers done when the widgets are obsolete?

The best reference materials are only a click away and time spent browsing the Internet will reap a lot of winning discoveries for today's marketplace.

So, if you are a trainer and no one comes out to class anymore, give training over the Internet. Hold meetings over the Internet. Perform support services over the Internet. In the throw-away appliance and electronic industry, the television repair business may not be so booming but the home theater business has plenty of room. And, just when you may be ready to throw in a towel on one business segment, there might be resurgence. Shoe repair businesses bustle when new shoe purchases start to be considered too frivolous.

We see examples all around us when we look at long-established businesses that are still thriving. The local butcher may no longer have yesterday's lure, having to compete with today's high-end supermarkets. Replacing the old product line with organic produce, niche products, dinners to go, and delivery service may do the trick. And, with an increase in senior citizens arriving, can you gear your practice to an older clientele? If various therapies, driving services, insurance claim help, and nursing assistance can replace some of your tired offerings, there is an aging population to address.

Searching the Internet for your own business model will give you other owners' ideas on new business offerings that they have found. The trick is never to let your business sit still and to constantly reinvent your model to meet a modern market.

Decreasing Expenses

Although most people don't think they are actually dumping money into the garbage, there is usually an ongoing "we've always done it like this" behavior pattern in a business. Checking for better pricing and reviewing to discover whether a need still exists more often than not gets trumped by the fires that need to be put out in the normal work day.

Here are some up-to-date reasons for checking every business expense on a frequent basis.

The Office

Overhead greatly influences the bottom line and yet many businesses never take the time to look for alternatives. Just starting a purchase order approval policy sometimes shines light on spending that you don't really need or pricing that needs to be checked. It sometimes just takes another set of eyes to spot the need for a change.

In a depressed real estate market, for example, rents become negotiable. For owners, real estate tax appeals on depressed values are on the rise.

It is also a buyer's market in many areas where monopolies used to exist.

Telephone costs, for instance, are plummeting and checking wireless, Internet, and land line costs once a year is not good enough any more. On almost a monthly basis, new group plans and competitive all-in-one deals are being introduced. Third-party companies will pick apart the phone bill you have paid for ten years, uncovering lines no longer used and expensive add-on-services that are free with other vendors.

Even when there is a credit crunch, paying penalties, late fees, and expensive credit card interest can possibly be managed with a more cost-effective loan.

Basically, every office expense should be listed for price checking every few months.

The cost of some outside services, such as payroll and payroll tax preparation, for instance, has also gone into freefall. Asking for a discount from just the largest national outside payroll companies can save you money, and you can save even more when you check for competitive pricing.

And, if the cost of on-site service and employee's time wasn't enough of an impetus for change in the past, outsourcing web-site hosting, email hosting, hardware maintenance, and system backups has become so cost effective and competitive that setting up and revisiting the pricing models every few months should be a top ten must-do.

Insurance-wise, even though most insurance costs keep climbing, the available menu of alternative plans keeps widening. There are many segments of insurance, however, that actually have reduced rates, such as professional liability and employee practices in certain fields.

Office expense staples of the past, such as equipment repair policies, may no longer be needed if the price of repair exceeds the price of replacement. And, is the postage meter used that much any more? With email and faxing overtaking the U.S. mail, that meter may be obsolete and its leased expense may be a waste of money.

Employee travel costs, possibly in effect since the business began, need scrutiny. Using cell phones and aircard Internet is far more cost effective than using the pricey hotel equivalents.

The trick is to put in place a strong review process and to have these types of cost-checks written right into someone's job description. And, on a more day-to-day note, it also doesn't hurt to turn out the lights and to adjust the thermostat after everyone goes home!

Decreasing Expenses

Cost of Goods

When a sale to a client includes something with hard costs, competition dictates that you better have the best product with the best price. Even for service businesses, there are often goods being sold. There isn't a manufacturer around that shouldn't have their prices checked. This may be old news for an owner and certainly for a salesperson, working on commission. However, thinking can be stale; methods change; the markets change. What went on a decade ago may not be all there is to know about costing the goods that you need to sell today.

Of course, there is the Internet. Many wholesalers sell directly, and sometimes under more than one brand name. So, if you buy through a distributor, you need to price-check with the manufacturer. And, if your customers can also buy directly, you need to cross-check their prices so that you have all of the facts before you lose credibility. Even the longest successful relationships you have had with vendors should be evaluated. And, some vendors offer price benefits when you limit your sales to just their product, eliminating your own offering of competitive labels. Many co-op refund programs and price reduction programs are written deeply into a vendor's marketing material—hard to find, posted in obscure website areas. Here again, vendor relations and price point-checking should be in someone's job description.

And do you really need clients finding holes in the packages you are offering? Just because your solution has included, with a price, a certain feature for umpteen years does not mean this is still the best, most modern alternative. Just as cell phones now come fully equipped with call forwarding, conferencing, and voice mail features that were separately priced in yesterday's phone markets, newer business software also comes out of the box with included features that used to cost more, when purchased separately, in the past. That expensive off-site training program, too, may be a thing of the past. Online e-learning tools are much more cost effective in terms of employee time and even free of charge in many cases. Staying ahead of the pack also has to include not only price-checking but freebie-checking. What have you have been including as a costed item that your customers can now get elsewhere free of charge? Maybe there is a better service feature, such as free Q&A or free online help that will list better on a feature list.

The trick here is having the best cost for the most attractive product and then concentrating on selling the service that you are actually in the business of selling.

The Workforce

For service providers, there has to be an optimum correlation between what customers will pay and what can thus be paid to the providers of the actual service. If, for instance, an employee's salary, tax contribution, and benefit contribution plus the factored-in overhead cost can't be covered by the price of the service you provide, well then, unless this service is used as a "loss leader," it has to be scrapped.

Pursuing excellence in the workforce plus keeping costs down in order to be competitive can be a juggling act, compounded greatly by an ever-changing technological world.

Assuming that you must have the right workers, at the right salary, performing the service you provide at the most marketable rates, the biggest challenge to a profitable model, and the challenge most affected by technological change, is the back office.

On one hand, we have an aging workforce, where computer use is not always fully embraced. There may be a tendency toward manual processes, certainly more telephone communication and even (ouch) letter writing. Then there is the younger worker who has an intuitive, life-long affinity with technology. This generation of workers uses the Internet for everything—texts and emails all day long, possibly listening to music at the same time. So, having employees with wisdom and career experience, but with dated costly methods is in direct contrast to having less experience in a workforce of multitasking, high-tech, less costly employees.

What is an owner to do? Certainly, being competitive in the marketplace, producing superior service, and still making profit is the goal. And, after finding just the right ratio between service provider salaries and the marketable price-point that your customers will pay, you can't just throw out the remaining profit. No one is served with a company going out of business.

Layoff discussions aside, the owner must grab the reins and, on behalf of the company's future, be lean and mean. It is the owner's duty to remove all of the roadblocks to competition that a nontechnological, nonchanging workforce creates, but still protect the business from decisions and actions that an inexperienced back office can produce.

So, decreasing costs may very well include a combination of higher-tech workers being groomed for more managerial decision making as well as more experienced, lower-tech personnel being force-fed the technological training needed.

Thirty years ago, attorneys didn't type. They dictated everything and spent their research hours surrounded by stacks of law books. Today's attorney must not only be proficient using online research tools, but must also be an extremely sophisticated word-processing user. New labor-saving tools need to be embraced even by the old guard. Luckily, training at every level is not as expensive as it was in the past and most vendor online training tools are even free. An employee trying to conquer the new tools of the trade can do so at any hour, repetitively, until the task is mastered.

The trick here is to do what is needed to protect profit, stay competitive, and still retain senior employees with the proper "store-watching" wisdom.

Streamlining Administration

There is only so much trimming of costs that can be done when part of your service solution is a product that you don't manufacture. You can only get the best price available for the certain component that you need to include. So, costs of goods in your pricing model may not have very much wiggle room. Similarly, if you need excellent service providers, there will more than likely be a salary range that you can't escape. You may require a certain level of employee with industry-standard experience and certification. That will carry a price tag and it will need to be paid. So, keeping costs down points in one direction—overhead. If you, indeed, have sales, and if you, indeed, cost your goods and your service providers' salaries properly, you should have profit. And, if you, indeed, have profit, you need to keep it.

After you have checked every expense that you pay in the office and staying as lean and mean as possible at every opportunity, there are some administrative changes that can further reduce expense and help boost the bottom line. I discuss these next.

Computerizing

Just as the workforce has to be computer literate, most small to mid-sized businesses will benefit greatly by being fully automated. A computer system purchase should be measured, not as an expense that has to be borne, but with a complete return on investment (ROI) analysis. Many software vendors provide ROI analytical tools and the results are eye-opening. And, not only should computer software be used to track receivable and payable records but having up-to-the-minute Profit and Loss information can make the difference between staying in business and going out of business.

Administrative staffs can be trimmed, profits can be micromanaged, potential sales can be tracked, and service providers' time can be optimized with a strong, stable, state-of-the-art computer solution.

Any business with multiple employees, a few year's longevity, and $1 million in revenue or more that does not have a computer system is a rarity. The benefits far outweigh the costs and, with hardware pricing shrinking by the day, along with easy-to-obtain vendor leasing plans, benefits can be immediately realized.

So, how would a classic service business benefit so greatly from a computer system? What's the big deal?

First of all, every computer system is not created equal. There are systems small and large but only a few specialists, such as physicians and attorneys, need anything proprietary or nongeneric. Large, national, or international software vendors with years invested in developing software have the most to offer and will have the best track record for future benefits.

Offering the greatest benefit to service businesses using software are three systems:

1. **Job Costing**. Income and expense is categorized on a job-by-job basis in order to measure profitability.
2. **Time and Billing.** Every service provider's day is broken up into the time they spent on every job and then labor costs are included in Job Costing.
3. **Customer Relationship Management (CRM).** Every customer and every prospective customer is managed and tracked for sales potential.

Although a business can spend an inordinate amount of money getting their accounting functions completed manually, tracking job profitability, equating employee labor and cost of goods to a customer sale, and tracking the activity of old and possibly new customers are usually the three areas that don't get done manually, despite the obvious need.

With a completely integrated computer system, an owner can reduce administrative labor, watch profits and losses extremely closely, track salesperson activity, and proactively interact with clients and prospective clients. And, when it costs only the equivalent of a monthly car payment, every owner should completely automate his or her back office functions immediately.

Given as a bonus, in addition to the Job Costing, Time and Billing, and Customer Relationship Management, are all the computer functions that people usually think of first—Receivables, Payables, Purchase Orders, Sales Orders, and General

Ledger. As important as these accounting functions are, automating them won't have as much effect on the bottom line as tackling the real profit boosters that compare labor and purchasing to the actual client sale.

Construction companies, for example, have costed their jobs since the beginning of their industry. They couldn't stay in business very long if they didn't allocate goods and labor to each job and walk away with a profit. Now if a computer consulting firm performs that same function—measuring each job's sale price versus the goods and labor that were provided—profit requirements would become more visible and play a higher role in pricing.

Similarly, law firms have "grown up" on billable hours and, with labor as their sole resource, usually get the procedure down pat for breaking down a day's work. Partners will know how many associates billed 2,000 hours last year and whether 50 or 60 hours, say, were needed to bill clients for a full 40-hour week. Now, if a landscape business or a plumbing business or any service business established this same billable hour mindset, in essence, everyone in the business would be helping to make a profit.

And, as with job profits and employee deliverables, "writing down" new sales opportunities can produce astonishing results. A salesperson will be very familiar with calling, say, 20 new prospects to get, perhaps, five sales appointments which will result, hopefully, in one new sale. However this information is being tracked, if a salesperson stays in the business of selling, you can rest assured that the tracking is being done. But if a person in the business of sales is supposed to keep tabs on potential new business, what about the tracking to be done by nonselling employees—the ones who are face-to-face with clients all week? Did the client mention that they hoped to have more training sessions next month or that they hoped to remodel next fall? Having a process in place for every employee to record the potential sales opportunities that they hear about in their normal course of business results in a nice big list of sales leads.

The trick here is to go for the gold: Get the proper profit-making tools for the proper business; get the whole system, implement it, live by it, cut unnecessary administrative costs, and reap the benefits of knowing what your true profit is as soon as possible.

Outsourcing

If there are specialized tasks that a small to mid-sized business does in-house that aren't directly related to servicing clients, perhaps the tasks should be outsourced. We've already mentioned outsourcing payroll and payroll tax preparation, as well as website hosting, email hosting, system backups, and even hardware maintenance checks.

What other tedious, time-consuming administrative functions are being performed by employees and is this the most cost-effective use of company dollars?

Almost anything to do with computer hardware, system security, and operating system upgrades is best serviced under maintenance contracts with outsourced hardware vendors. Even some complex computer software and report-writing applications are more cost-effectively managed out-of-house by appropriate experts. Website development and all forms of electronic buying and selling (Ecommerce and Electronic Data Interchange [EDI]) will, more often than not, require excessive training and in-house resources that outsourcing will avoid.

Another natural for outsourcing is advanced marketing where the expertise of an outside public relations firm may be better used on an hourly basis than trying to maintain the same high standard with an in-house employee. Outsourced costs for press releases, ads, newsletters, mass emails, direct mailers, and even telemarketing functions are hard to beat dollar for dollar when absorbed internally by administrative staff. Where once it may have been cost effective to perform many of these functions in-house, web-based alliances and automation have created a new level of competition, and it can do wonders to help your bottom line.

Even the most standard administrative tasks can be outsourced using today's technology. "Virtual Assistants," for instance, are today's personal secretaries, working remotely but handling all types of administrative, data entry, and professional assistance.

If outsourcing seems far-fetched and you can't imagine running a business without an office full of employees performing various administrative functions, just look at completely "virtual businesses" that you use and respect.

Have you bought anything from Amazon lately? Wasn't the service great? You saw the availability of inventory, were invoiced, given a ship date and a tracking number for your order. Have you downloaded music lately? Visited iTunes? Downloaded a movie? These businesses don't occupy space in the mall and have automated almost every aspect of their service. Yes, you need to perform the service that your customers require and perhaps you won't have a completely empty office but you can streamline more of your administration. Step one would be to automate all that is possible. Step two would be to outsource non-client-specific tasks that may be bogging the business down.

The trick is to revolve the service business around servicing clients and generating sales and to outsource administrative-heavy tasks that are more cost-effectively performed by outside specialists.

Standardizing

A real crime that many small to mid-sized businesses commit is reinventing the wheel for every client, for every sale, and for every problem. Just like an operational manual will teach the universe of purchasers how to use a new product, if the office doesn't set down some rules of order, every person will use their best judgment (or lack of best judgment) to perform services, close sales and, even, set pricing.

Even though, in theory, all businesses have rules, they sometimes aren't passed along to new employees; new situations aren't equated to old situations and the new interfacing of personal and business lives tests old boundaries.

An office manual, as mundane as it sounds, not only helps productivity but can also serve as a problem-solving client relationship guide without excessive back-and-forth among everyone in the office.

Stepping back a moment and documenting these business processes will optimize productivity, reduce redundant discovery, improve customer relations, and improve the bottom line.

For employees:

- Dress code
- Start time and end time
- Vacation and personal time policy
- Benefit package
- Employment agreement
- Client check lists
- Client follow up policy
- Job deliverables
- Weekly reporting requirements
- Office policy on computer, phone, and equipment use
- Security protocol
- Ongoing training
- Hiring practices
- Idea generation

For clients:

- Sales techniques
- Proposal standards
- Contract standards
- Pricing policy
- Collection practices
- Product and service descriptions
- Problem resolution policy
- Customer service policy

For administration:

- Vendor and client contact information
- Job descriptions
- Reporting requirements and deliverable schedules
- Expense checking
- Vendor relationships
- Client relationships
- Marketing management
- Accounting requirements

The message is to standardize the office, commit to writing what is *assumed* to be policy, and remove the endless hours spent rethinking solutions which were analyzed and resolved long ago.

Taking a look at a franchise business or a national chain store, the standardizing is blatant. Starbucks looks pretty much the same and makes the same cup of coffee across the country. You can expect that your Dunkin' Donut will taste the same no matter where you buy it. Your small to mid-sized business can't afford to have its services reinvented every day.

The trick is to avoid the pitfalls discovered in the past and spend more time investing in repeating the company's successes.

Revamping

With computer technology, managing office functions and administrating a business have taken on a different life. Not only can work be done remotely, removing the need for everyone to occupy a desk and office space, but with email, the Internet, and sophisticated computer systems, much more work can be done in a shorter amount of time. We've already discussed the experienced, senior, lower-tech employee versus the inexperienced, junior, higher-tech employee. Also, outsourcing options may reduce or eliminate some in-house processes. There is, however, a whole other employee solution that directly boosts the bottom line at the same as it enhances the business model.

High level, highly paid, flexible part-time workers are more available than ever to perform many administrative functions reliably. Between stay-at-home parents with master's degrees and self-employed professionals of every size and shape, if you have not carefully analyzed what is being spent and what is being produced administratively in the office, it is time to do it now.

Managing Directors, Office Managers, Accountants, CFOs, CIOs, Sales Directors, and any other high-level managers that you can't afford or don't need on a full-time basis can be hired on a flexible, part-time basis.

A part-time, highly-skilled bookkeeper or accountant can set up depreciation tables, properly post accruals, and keep profit and loss information on an almost real-time schedule, keeping outside accounting fees at a minimum. How does this compare to the current back office staff? It is the same with many other management level administrator jobs where processes can be automated, remote monitoring can be established, and sophisticated computer programs can help do a lot of the grunt work.

Many primary caregivers for young children or older parents want to spend their business careers working part time or with flexible schedules as self-employed professionals. Paying a part-timer even three times the hourly rate that you have paid to lower-level employees may be extremely cost effective in the long run. As with a Virtual Assistant or in a virtual business model, there are many cost-effective, profit-oriented alternatives to hiring a full house of full-time, stationary administrators.

The trick here is to embrace automation and look into hiring staff with above-average capabilities on a mutually beneficial flexible schedule.

In Summary

Taking the common-sense approach, if you need to have more money in the bank at the end of the month, the first solution that comes to mind is to generate more sales. But without seriously trying to reduce expenses and tweak costly administrative processes, more money in could just as easily mean more money out!

So, while selling more is a natural goal, cost cutting and streamlining must go hand in hand with selling if greater profits are to be kept.

Increasing sales opportunities can include:

- Complementing your main offerings with additional products and services
- Turning one-time only business into ongoing relationships
- Creating vertical markets while still selling to the masses
- Changing your target audience
- Establishing "get in the door" programs
- Creating new business off-shoots
- Reinventing sales solutions

Decreasing expenses can include:

- Constantly reviewing all office spending
- Monitoring the right costs for the right goods being sold
- Mixing and matching the workforce

Streamlining administration can include:

- Computerizing all business functions
- Removing in-house efforts where outsourcing makes more sense
- Committing standard practices to writing
- Embracing a flexible workforce

These "clean up shop" tactics can be great morale boosters and can go a long way to turning around a business that has lost its profit focus.

Staying Visible and Connected

Goals

- Increase credentials
- Grow affiliations

Increasing Credentials

Just as taking a fresh look at a business's rules of operations will undoubtedly generate a need for change, taking the customer's view of why the business should be chosen over its competitors will also be an eye-opening experience. To reaffirm a company's credibility and differentiate it from the competition, you need to revisit the standard "emblems" that your field uses to validate skill, prove expertise, and market business credibility.

Going back to basics, a few simple questions need to have simple answers:

- What does your business do for a living?
- What do you need to know to do that job?
- How good are you?
- How good are your products and services?
- How do you stand out from your competitors?
- And, finally, how would a new customer know these answers?

For a long-standing business, the sign on the door may have at one point said it all—"Authorized Product X dealer" or "Certified Public Accountant," but times have changed and competition is everywhere. The respectable major brand logo on your business card representing some well-known alliance may not carry as much weight as it did in the past. Similarly, just meeting minimum standards in a field that has profession-wide credential requirements may no longer be good enough. "Attorney at Law" signs may be a dime a dozen in your town. Tired, old-fashioned, or even, lazy behavior on your part may leave the new kid on the block overflowing with the exact credits, licenses, and published accolades that your business should have rightfully earned.

There may be an almost pompous disregard by a long-standing business to measure up to the competition in a world with many new measurements. Fields like technology, finance, and health care have certifications and credentials that keep evolving. And, many other fields have newly-minted product and profession-wide designations that can boost a company's image, and, in an instant, help convey what a firm is all about.

If you dropped the ball and didn't beef up the company's resume, it's time to step back and see what credentials are missing and what the competitors flash around to nab the business that your firm should be handling.

So, if you want to look for new ways to let the world know who you are, here are a few areas to pounce on immediately.

The Basics

You can't practice medicine without a license and you can't practice law without passing the bar exam. You can, however, perform accounting services, be a chef in a restaurant, or install computer systems without taking any tests and without breaking any laws.

So, legal requirements aside, a service business owner has to measure the return on investment in obtaining some of the many professional and industry-wide certifications that are not mandated, but are available to establish credibility in the market space.

Now, if your business is all about "location, location, location" then you may be exempt from marketing your proficiencies or from demonstrating the superiority of your products. But, if you don't have a coffee shop or a shoe shine stand in bustling Penn Station, then the quality of the goods and the services that you provide needs to somehow stand on its own merits. Having "stamps of approval"—accreditations, licenses, and certifications—certainly goes a long way in at least winning a customer's attention and then, hopefully, their business.

The branding of excellence, in itself, is a big business where teaching, testing, and accreditation often come at a hefty price. Persistence and nonstop administrative effort is almost always required to bring the application for a highly coveted designation to fruition. It goes without saying that there must be a compelling reason to go to the extremes necessary to obtain a lot of designations and to maintain continued eligibility year after year. So, what "pieces of paper" or "badges of distinction" are worthy of your hard-earned time and money?

Well, you have a service business, maybe selling some products. If there are any mandated, governmental license requirements, these are, of course, first to be met. Next, if products are involved, are there any vendor-required certifications to be acquired? Are there levels? How far do you go? If a client is looking for an air-conditioning specialist and you represent that air-conditioning vendor, it behooves you to be as certified as you can be—the reseller, the repair center, the training center, the "Gold" dealer.

Besides vendors' product certifications, there are industry and profession-wide certifications to consider.

If you are a technology service company, for example, start with establishing all of the necessary credentials for any products that you sell or service in your solutions. All of the major technology vendors, such as Microsoft, Cisco, and SAP, have certification programs that will establish your firm as qualified to perform your service. When it comes to profession-wide accreditation, in this field, some of the more vendor-free designations won't have the marketable strength that the large recognizable product-geared stamps of excellence provide. So, it will be more common in a technology field to utilize, for example, Microsoft designations to convey profession-wide competency than to use some of the various system engineering accreditations that objective third parties can provide. The public knows the big products more than they know technical job classifications. So, product emblems here will also convey industry-wide power and might. The goal is to market your firm. So, if flashing major product credibility conveys the level of competency and professional pride that you are targeting, then this is the path to take.

For financial professionals, the reverse is true. An accounting firm will rarely be asked to establish competency in the various accounting systems or spreadsheets that they and their customers use. They will, however, be measured by profession-wide designations such as Certified Financial Planner (CFP) or Certified Public Accountant (CPA). In this field, niche operations such as auditing, fraud investigation, and wealth management are opportune areas where garnishing more credentials will let a company prove expertise and establish increased competency.

Vertical markets can be very demanding about qualifications when seeking to hire an accredited service-providing company with experience in their field. For example, perhaps you want to provide services to country clubs, college-bound seniors, or hospital administrators. By having "approved by," "certified by," "registered by," or "recommended by" designations that specifically address the vertical market, you will trump the marketing generalist who doesn't appear to have the specific, tailored skills to succeed.

And, if bigger is better, then so be it. If, for instance, you offer training and some of your potential students are accountants who can earn their license-required continuing education credits, you can become federally certified to issue these credits, not just state certified, and this can increase your potential audience.

If, in order to obtain any of these coveted certifications, there is training, related travel, and tests to be taken, how many of your employees should you involve? Should you add to your credentials by having different employees focus on different masteries? Will enhancing your credentials also result in sales leads and marketing rewards? If products are involved and you use various vendors, would there be a greater benefit to concentrating all your efforts with one vendor and a bigger one at that? Would it be easier to gain prominence, references, and greater market share by dealing with a new large national or international partner? Can co-op funds, realized from sales efforts, be used to afford further accreditations and marketing-geared recognition, such as press releases and advertisements?

What about free-standing associations, not involving employee expertise or any products sold or serviced?

Certain hotels, for instance, apply for membership in elite organizations, such as Relais & Chateaux or The Leading Hotels of the World, where a recognizable emblem will immediately convey a level of charm and excellence in both accommodations and cuisine.

The trick is to continually upgrade and reinvent your "business resume" and to arm your company with the marketing-based credentials that it deserves.

Awards

Certifications, accreditations, stamps of approval, and licenses present an aura of effort. You took the right tests; you sold enough goods; you had enough clients; you haven't done any harm.

Awards, on the other hand, appear to the public to have noncomplicity. People think you must be special to get an award, that everyone knows this, and, therefore, you deserve the accolades. In most business cases, however, awards are as hard-earned and labor-intensive as obtaining new certifications, and need even more cleverness and top-down effort to be researched, applied for, and, finally won. A business might strategize intently, lobby, pay advisors, and employ staff just to do what it takes to win a reputable, newsworthy award.

In vendor circles, there are Presidents Clubs, Third Party Product Developers of the Year, New Partner of the Year and Bronze, Gold or Platinum awards. Magazines, newspapers, and websites will issue Yearly Top 100 lists of all kinds; Business Associations will have Person of the Year, Business of the Year, or Innovator of the Year; charitable organizations may have Fundraiser of the Year or Philanthropist of the Year.

No matter what the award, the prestige and marketing power shines the business in a different light and sets it apart from its competitors.

Everyone wants to be with a winner, and, aside from a few surprises, the intense efforts that are usually required to measure up, apply, and then actually achieve an award must be well conceived and expertly executed.

Many times public relations firms will be involved in award discovery and nomination, but even without a PR firm, self-promotion can be organized and included in a few employees' job descriptions.

What business associations, such as women's business groups, Chambers of Commerce, or industry specific organizations, are you involved with and what awards do they announce?

What vendors do you deal with and do they reward more than just sales volume? Is there a Trainer of the Year Award, Customer Satisfaction Award, Customer Retention Award? Should you routinely ask for customer recommendations when you complete a job?

And, thinking doesn't have to be local or small. You may not have the qualifications to be on the Inc. 500 list or to have one of Time magazines Best Inventions of the Year—but you might. Businesses that reap national attention or top-notch local attention are catapulted into a new level of prominence. It is the first thing on the lips of everyone that you meet—"I saw you in the paper"; "Congratulations on your win."

So, part of your credential-gathering quest can include the quest for an award.

Restaurateurs and chefs will cherish a James Beard Foundation award; producers and directors will cherish their Oscars; athletes will cherish their gold medals; and your organization can equally cherish your Business of the Year award.

The trick here is to seek out avenues where you can put your qualifications and accomplishments on display and be acknowledged and rewarded for your success. Your website, your newsletter, and your company brochure will all spread your good news.

Employee Recognition

The advertising of the company's accomplishments, certifications, and awards is commonplace, and, given that you arm yourself with appropriate credentials, your company will be able to hold its own against the competition.

What is often a hidden, unexploited asset is the most valuable asset of a service firm—the workforce.

What is it about your staff that sets you apart from your competitors?

If you are a law firm, do you have any Certified Trial Attorneys? If you are an accounting firm, how many of your employees are CPAs? If you support computer hardware, how many members of your technical staff hold Microsoft or other vendors' certifications?

Do you have PhDs on staff? How many college graduates or certified technicians do you employ? How many years of experience do your employees have? In what fields? With what success?

How many of your employees have longevity at your own firm? Is their commitment to your company, in itself, a statement about your firm's competency and attractiveness?

Do you have strong connections with any of your employees' alma maters? Did your employees garnish their own awards in previous careers or while in school?

More appealing to employees, sometimes, than bragging about their business credentials is bragging about their weekend warrior conquests—their golf game, the marathon they ran, the triathlon they conquered, and even their children's accolades.

Sponsoring softball teams, matching funds for charitable fundraising events, and becoming involved in many other employee-driven personal interests create a business image that "isn't all business." Your website, your in-house newsletter, and your clients' newsletter are all perfect vehicles for this kind of employee-based news. And, whether you use the individual bios of your staff members or the collective company-wide stats about the strengths of your workforce, what you want to convey is a wholesome, attractive view of what is beneath the surface of your firm.

In fashion circles, pretty faces will be used to help market pretty clothes to consumers. Eileen Fisher, a clothing retailer, uses their own company employees in ads where the employees' casual, natural beauty happens to also describe the clothing line. In your service business, having a capable, highly certified, experienced, and interesting staff is not something that should be hidden.

And, an employee's business resume should be enhanced not only when they are job searching. Creating a path of ongoing training, certification seeking, and award collecting can be as personally motivating to an employee as it is beneficial to the company.

The trick is to involve employees in the acceleration and touting of their accomplishments. The strength of the work-force in a service-based business is a major asset in the company's profile.

Growing Affiliations

With the most competitive credentials in hand for the company and the staff, a quick look at all association memberships and ongoing alliances can help refocus and modernize the business network chain.

Sometimes, unfortunately, growing alliances in a well-established business really means "out with the old and in with the new."

So, why are affiliations so important? Shouldn't marketing and sales efforts, alone, keep the bottom line bubbling? Does a company really need to belong to any associations or enter into any ongoing alliances?

The seasoned owner can get a lot out of taking a hard look at how the business's reference base began—was it fueled by local business connections, golfing friends, vendor leads, strangers seeing ads?

The business was built on some form of networking that worked. Has this model been visited lately? Are the age-old memberships and connections stale and out-of-touch? Do newer businesses, with perhaps virtual connections, have a distinct advantage over your long-established firm? Things have changed, but what's new? What should be kept in place and what needs to be revamped?

The goal is to put a face on your business that outsiders will recognize. Then, after building up credentials of all kinds, establish and grow a basic alliance network that will be seamless and automatic in enhancing sales.

Here are a few areas that can modernize and grow today's service business alliances.

Traditional Associations

Assuming that you have joined traditional associations over the years, some questions need to be answered:

- For how many associations is your company paying dues?
- What is the value of each membership?
- Are you an active member, with continuing involvement?
- Do you generate any business or other benefit from the membership?
- Did you reap great benefit from involvement in the past and want to, thus, continue only as a valued supporter?

Starting with Chambers of Commerce, a service business might have many local, county, state, and even national memberships. There might be various business and professional organizations, political or lobbying types of groups, and ethnic, gender, and alumni connections, all of which you belong to now or have in the past. Vendor and job-oriented user and peer groups, as well as industry-specific groups for your own and your clients' businesses may be on your list. You may be a member of a horizontally geared group, such as an association for manufacturers, or a tight vertical organization such as a food wholesaler association. Every client you ever dealt with could have pointed you in the direction of a trade association.

When all is said and done, you could have a lot of associations generating dues from your check registry where you have little or no involvement and reap no benefits.

If a business chooses a few traditional associations, of course, the greatest benefits come from being active, being known, and becoming friends with members. So, if attending meetings, joining committees, working on association boards, and attending networking cocktail parties is a thing of the past in your business plan, so too are probably most traditional association memberships.

You may still benefit from some of these connections—preparing presentations, attending annual conferences, writing newsletter articles, and, in general, being known. But, if the hand-shaking type of networking is what a group is all about, and if you aren't present and accounted for, it's time to move on.

Small to mid-sized businesses need to gain specific benefits from association memberships of any kind. Whether the association is local or national, whether it represents your own business's industry or that of your potential clients—what you join, what benefits you expect, and what benefits you reap need to be evaluated.

The trick with business associations is to maintain the ones that are valuable, eliminate the ineffective ones, and invest your efforts in alliances that are most valuable and pertinent in today's business model.

Strategic Alliances

Pointed, reliable, and representative of a wider marketplace, today's strategic alliances are like cogs in a wheel.

You may be an automatic part of someone else's solution today and tomorrow they may become an automatic part of your solution. You may be riding someone else's coattails today, returning the favor tomorrow.

The Internet, of course, has changed the game and, although there is nothing new about referrals or service bundling or subcontracting or any other kind of partnering, a solution today—even a service solution—can easily contain a component provided by someone hundreds of miles away.

Depending on your service offering, where can you fit into a grander solution provided by others? Can you provide training for all technical installations, or clean up after plumbing fiascos? Can your firm be the trusted advisor for small business centers in your state, or provide document storage functions for an accounting firm and its clients? Looking at it in reverse, who can be utilized to augment your solution? Can remote access possibilities enlarge your offerings and help you create a more aggressive sales model?

With Google, Wikipedia, Bing, and Yahoo, you can find innumerable examples of pertinent alliance building and then with the help of your vendors, your peers, and your competitors' websites, your research can lead you to the strategic alliances that will best suit your firm. When you become part of a solution that someone else is selling, your business can take a leap that your old one-to-one sales tactic could not possibly have matched.

Strategic alliances can also serve marketing purposes when you establish an ongoing, respected network with traditional and online newspapers, magazines, and even television networks.

Could you be one of those television experts that are called to comment on various industry issues? If you are a technologist, for example, can you be the voice of the technology community when a quote is needed? And, the same goes for all types of experts. Especially on cable television, talking heads presenting the pros and cons on countless topics are needed 24/7.

Can you write a weekly column for an online newspaper or magazine? Can you have it syndicated and automatically included in association newsletters or other relevant online sites? Once you become a guest expert in either a traditional or online forum, your name will pop up over and over again when opinions are sought.

The trick is to take your show on the road, and establish strategic connections that you hadn't pursued or that weren't even available in the past. The Internet, along with more traditional outlets, can expand your audience and build a new foundation in networking.

New Tactics

Crossing over into the land of marketing, growing affiliations of all kinds can help you advertise, and can help you sell. The point of revisiting old networking tactics is to stop wasting time and money and to capitalize on what technology has brought to the table—the masses.

Everyone is online. Therefore, your business must be online. If you concentrate solely on old-fashioned networking methods, you leave the web game in the hands of your competitors who may or may not be better service performers than you are, but with their better online tactics, they will appear to be.

One of the first new concepts to learn about networking online is ad sharing. You want your website to be visited and referred. Basically you want your traffic to be increased. So you can point to other businesses, display relevant corporate ads and, create a bigger, broader look for your business. Checking some of the Google Ad areas will show you what's possible and, at least, help you see what the competition is doing.

Using analytical tools on your website will also tell you where people come from when they visit your site. If you have your name on vendor sites, alliance sites, or in advertising arenas, you can use Google Analytics to identify the links that people are using to get to your site.

Affiliate Marketing is a new buzz term and is more marketing oriented than some of these other networking processes. In Affiliate Marketing, a customer visits a website, is sent to your website, and then signs up for your services. This isn't that different from calling a dentist and asking for a referral to an orthodontist, for example, but on the web the possibilities are endless. Your accounting firm can be referred to in people's articles about tax preparation, or on an accounting software site, or on a women-owned business forum. And, these new alliance-building techniques are changing and growing by the day.

Perhaps the most startling change in alliance building in history has come from social network sites, such as Facebook and MySpace, where hundreds of millions of people connect with each other in an ever-expanding web of connectivity. Relationships that would have been short-lived in another time are preserved and extended through these sites.

Similar network sites exist and are gaining ground in the business world. LinkedIn, for instance, is a networking site where companies and professionals connect with business peers, potential clients, and personal friends. Just by connecting to one person, you can network to that person's connections and so on and so on. Your new "network" can be used for business opportunities, job searches, recommendations, and introductions.

If time and money is to be invested in networking activity, how can these sites with hundreds of millions of members be ignored? Welcome to the online business community.

And, if words like traffic, links, and analytics seem foreign to you, or if you are not familiar with sites like LinkedIn, Facebook, Bing, and Google, a trip to the local bookstore is needed.

The trick is to recognize where business networking is going, and to be able to change gears—quickly.

In Summary

Whenever a new business takes shape, an owner will be in marketing mode, aiming to create networks, establish credibility, and win over prospective clients.

Keeping a client base and staying afloat year after year may cause a business to rest on its laurels and stop doing the reality checks necessary to stay on top of the game.

If profits are slipping and the business is getting an overhaul, revisiting the certifications that are essential to compete and the associations that can keep business coming in will shed new light on sprucing up a tired model.

Increasing a company's credentials can include:

- Updating a business' resume with marketing-geared accreditations
- Seeking recognition through awards
- Touting the strengths and advantages of the workforce

Growing affiliations can include:

- Eliminating stale, ineffective alliances
- Establishing new Internet-based affiliations, as well as maintaining traditional strategic alliances
- Creating online marketing and business networks

These back-to-basics strategies are geared to refurbishing what might be a stale set of certifications and associations. With an updated business "face" and a newly enhanced alliance platform, new business opportunities will begin to present themselves.

Maximizing Cash Flow

Goals

- Keep cash flowing
- Know your budget
- Work to the bottom line

Keeping the Cash Flowing

Whether the bottom line is red or black, cash flow is the major concern of every small to mid-sized business. Personal money may, often, flow in and out of a privately held business to help the cause but, if the crux of the problem is lack of real profit, it will surely consistently continue to manifest itself in one area— cash flow.

So, there is no money coming in; the owner has no idea when money will arrive and anxiously waits for the mail every day or, worse yet, hopelessly waits for any sign of a new customer who will save the day or save the payroll. Can a different model be set up? Can the same service business redesign itself with a more favorable cash flow situation that will ultimately help create a more favorable profit situation? Here are a few tried and true ideas to improve the management of the service business around the flow of cash.

Retainer Plans

In a service business, there is some labor being performed. What is it? Is it bundled with product delivery or does it stand alone? When working toward a relationship sales model, the whole idea is to avoid one-time, nonrepetitive sales at all costs. And, when working toward a better cash flow situation, the whole idea is to avoid a large Accounts Receivable balance.

Probably out of fear of never being paid, a whole subset of service businesses have grown to rely on prepaid retainer plans. Certainly attorneys, computer consultants, and architects commonly require retainers. However, almost every service business can design a model where a retainer plan is beneficial to the client, and at the same time is a cash flow savior to the business itself.

Starting from scratch, you meet a new client, you present a proposal, and you include a retainer plan. Maybe it is for the anticipated labor to do the architectural drawings or for the investigation of a legal matter or just to be on call for any technical problems. In any case, a series of fixed priced projects gets removed from the retainer plan, hourly labor costs are deducted, or a certain number of prefixed service calls are covered. The beauty of working with retainer plans is that they can be renewable. The work being done is capped by the retainer plan and then a supplemental plan is sold when the original plan is finished.

Ongoing plans with automatic credit card payments are so common in so many industries that you have to wonder why it would be any different in most service businesses. Health clubs, diet centers, cable television companies, email hosting centers, and an endless list of other business types survive every month by dipping into our credit cards for prepayment. If you do not have this model in place, it is time to rethink your sales offerings to incorporate cost-effective and cash-flow-efficient retainer plans.

So, what are the sales benefits when switching from a net 30 business model to a retainer plan model? How could a customer possibly find value in this new arrangement?

Switching an entire client base to prepaid retainers can be a long process, but is still very doable. The values to the client have to be convincing and real. You may also have to have intermediary "baby" steps, but your goal can be 100% integration into retainer billing.

First of all, retainers can guarantee rates for x amount of months or years. Prepaying a year's fee or just x amount of labor hours allows the customer to budget costs that will not change for the length of the retainer.

If an agreement allowing for net 30 terms had certain minimum charges, such as two-hour visits, larger purchase requirements, or overtime charges for after-hours work, these caveats can be removed in the retainer plan. Hot lines, immediate help, priority scheduling, and off-hour guaranteed assistance are all hot buttons that create value for a customer in a retainer agreement.

The most important part of using this structure is to set it up with fair and competitive guidelines and then stick by it. There can be no wavering. It has to represent your business model in order to be effectively sold.

Some common retainer-oriented fields where customers have learned to accept this structure without question include financial advising, marketing assistance, web development, computer support, estate planning, college counseling, and more.

Sole proprietors and freelancers have a strong need to ensure cash flow and payment for their services, thus requiring and asking, many times, for payment in advance. However, even the largest players in many service fields manage entire books of business with retainer billing.

Part of an owner's lean and mean strategy, which helps to keep costs down for customers, allows the hiring of the proper number of support staff to precisely match the needs of clients who are retainer engaged.

In some cases, businesses already have a model where they start with prebilling, then choose to invoice on terms in the future. However user-friendly this may be, the essence of planning for a steady cash influx is best served by engaging all clients in ongoing retainer plans. Always remember that no client ever benefits when the business has to close its doors so setting up a model that keeps a business financially healthy is the owner's responsibility.

If a business has never operated in this fashion and has steady cash flow problems, it is time to consider a revamp.

Several retainer models offer varying degrees of labor rates and "included benefits," dependent on the size of the prepaid contracts. So, the smallest retainer (most like a one-time sale) would have to carry the highest labor price per hour or service fee to the customer and the least amount of extra benefits. By changing, for example, a full-priced 8-hour labor charge to a more discounted 10-hour retainer plan, you do the following:

- Establish a relationship.
- Engage your client in the model that serves your business best.

Without truly analyzing this model, it may seem that charging someone, say, $100 per hour on a 10-hour retainer plan would not be as profitable as charging the going rate of $125 per hour for a one-shot eight-hour job. But, relationships are what keep a service business's doors open. The same $1,000 for the 10-hour retainer plan makes your lower hourly rate cost-competitive. It also leaves the client, who initially required only eight hours of services, with two remaining hours to be used for services in the future. This opens the door for the client to call again and for you to reach out to the client. The next request will rarely stop at two hours and will keep the relationship open for more and more services to be provided.

The trick here is to package services in prepaid bundles, creating a reliable customer base that can be serviced more cost-effectively. For the naysayer, you only need to look at all of the services you rely on personally and remember how you pay for them. The gym does not accept payment after you have finished your workout, the cable company bills before you get to view their channels, and many a home service provider demands prepayment before beginning their job.

Retainer plans will go a long way in stabilizing a service business's all-consuming, never-ending battle with cash flow.

Maintenance Contracts

When the furnace breaks down, a pipe leaks, or the new PC won't boot up, we are fairly comfortable with the concept of using a maintenance contract that has been prepaid annually, year after year. But more and more industries are setting up required maintenance contracts for home and office repair, alarm maintenance, quarterly tax services, and other needed, but sporadically scheduled services. It is the "right to call," the expectation to receive prompt help, and the guarantee that your needs will be met that generates a call to action to sign up in advance for many of these contracts.

Many service businesses that have never considered maintenance contracts can start a whole new revenue stream, and at the same time offer clients responsive or proactive, less expensive, needed services.

Starting with home repair services, the landscaper, the sprinkler technician, the swimming pool caretaker, the tree pruner, the pest controller; the HVAC, plumbing, and electrical service techs; and fireplace, computer, appliance, communications and "handyman" help are all fields where maintenance contracts are quasi-mandatory. So, if even one of these service providers can establish a practice with a maintenance contract requirement, why can't others?

For business-to-business services, the office owner or building manager may actually be more inclined to engage in many of the same repair and maintenance types of contracts listed above for a home. There is a strong need in an office to keep everything working. So, having contracts in place for on-call help is a must. But, additionally, contracts for computer software help, hardware service, virus protection, and system updates are now standard office requirements.

Proactive support, possibly saving serious reactive support dollars, certainly sells many a new contract, but the biggest customer benefit is being connected to the right company that can give the customer the help they need when they need it. For the service-providing firm, the biggest benefit is knowing how many customers you have, how much work you can expect to do, and how much cash you can expect to have flowing through your doors.

The trick is to create maintenance contracts that meet a client's needs for both proactive and reactive support, as well as the business's need for better cash planning.

Working with the Calendar

Another aspect of what has grown to become normal in this area is the once-a-year or once-a-month contract renewal process. Whether it is identified as a registration fee, a maintenance fee, a subscription fee, or a usage fee, the fee itself is all around us.

If you go online and want to read the latest detailed college rankings or the comparison of all Zagat-rated restaurants, you can't just view once for a small fee or pay later. You have to subscribe for x amount of time (i.e., pay the subscription price). The impulsive sign-up most often comes with an automatic renewal, requiring a cancellation, in writing. Even your fancy credit card will collect a yearly fee just so you have the right to charge purchases. Of course, bundling "platinum" or "gold" benefits helps to make the credit card fee more palatable.

When software programs are purchased, a yearly license or maintenance fee will ensure delivery of any needed software repairs or updates. In this case, these yearly fees, costing about 20% of the original product's purchase price, in essence create the same value as a brand new sale for the vendor every five years.

So, fees are everywhere, and, if the service business builds a repertoire of services wrapped around weekly, monthly, or yearly prepaid fees, the fees can be set up to be paid in slow cash flow months or, at least, at consistent times.

Many contract sellers will prorate your sign-up so that you are on the January renewal schedule or the first of the month billing cycle. In any case, these are scheduling opportunities that can assist in cash flow control.

Wearing the marketing hat at the same time as the cash flow hat allows a business to push certain things at year-end, before a "new year price increase," or in the winter before the lawn-care season begins, and so on.

The trick is to look at any recurring-fee model that fits your service business, establish the fee and at the same time work with the calendar to generate this income at traditional cash-flow-shy times of the month or year.

Managing the Workload

Assuming that each service company is in the business of performing excellent service, staying in business over the long run is about dollars and cents. If payroll is to be met, bills are to be paid, and customers are to remain happy, there has to be a respect for cash flow when managing the workload.

For instance, if everything is literally dropped to sign up a new customer, as many times happens, the same level of attention that is directed at the new "money in the bank" has to be applied to work schedules. Barring emergencies, service providers need to have schedules that bring them to the next payment phase of a contract or the next prepaid contract renewal point. There is a science to managing this type of service performance in a business and proper Monday-morning reporting can enable a manager to assign work around optimum payment generation.

If working entirely on installing a brand new swimming pool in a backyard suspends everyone else's weekly pool cleaning service and, thus, the next prepayments for 50 weekly customers, well, that is not a good plan. So, the big new installation needs to be properly scheduled and stretched out, satisfying the 50 valued clients and maintaining the cash flow that this represents.

However, the big new swimming pool job may carry a significant influx of cash, so maybe extra work hours need to be scheduled or more of the weekly maintenance customers need to be handled within each work day to satisfy all clients. Picking and choosing what work is done on a given day cannot be done in a vacuum. Cash needs and potential payments need to be combined to create the healthiest possible combination of customer satisfaction and financial stability.

The trick is to have access to all of the knowledge that lets this sophisticated type of scheduling be done. Just as a manufacturer's shop floor scheduling system will manage available labor and materials against open sales orders and required shipping dates, a service company must manage producers' efforts with respect to clients' demands and cash flow requirements.

Scheduling Vendor and Cross-Selling Income

For a service business, any income derived from the sale of goods might or might not be a major revenue source.

Nonetheless, when goods are ordered, it helps to bring cash flow into the equation. Things like credit card statement dates, vendor salesperson's commission schedules, and, even, your own commission schedules should be recognized as important parts of the entire vendor relationship.

For instance, if you order a large number of items and must pay in full for these items, you should be cognizant of your own credit card statement date, allowing the maximum in credit terms. If the end of a quarter or the end of a month boosts the vendor's salesperson's commission, you might reap some benefits by waiting to place an order until the last day of a certain cycle and, thus, gain a few extra month-end discount dollars. So, your own sale of any goods should keep your own payments and costs in mind.

Similarly, when cross-selling goods and services to your customers, you can maximize your profits and minimize your expense by scheduling the sale and the accompanying income to meet low-cash-flow-periods, especially if they can coincide with a vendor's slow time, reaping better profit margins.

Some service providers even resell low-profit margin goods purely for the attractiveness of the cash flow. Selling a PC, for instance, to your service-only customer may bring pennies in profit but can provide a cash float of 30 days or longer between the customer's order date and the vendor's payment date.

Many times, service businesses do not pay enough attention to the residual commissions that they are owed for their cross-selling efforts. Anticipated referral fees, vendor co-op fees, and actual sales commissions are usually not entered into a company's Accounts Receivable system and, thus, arrive in the mail as "surprise" checks. However, with vendors themselves being bought and sold, the relationships (and ensuing cash income) that you have established in your cross-selling model must be preserved, valued, revisited, and expected.

The trick here is to manage all income derived from commissions or vendor programs and to purchase and order goods with a respect for cash flow and credit availability.

Credit Planning

Paying bills, especially when cash is tight, keeps many a worried owner awake at night. Besides payroll, the IRS, rent and utilities, insurances, and vendors all demand prompt payment satisfaction or cancellations will ensue.

For the richest businesses credit planning might not matter as much. but for the usual small to mid-sized firms—where economic pressures are felt first and relief is felt last—cash flow management cannot be successful without attention to credit.

Credit crunches aside, handling every item in Accounts Payable with a sophisticated eye can reduce late fees, penalties, credit card expense, and other dreaded, unnecessarily lost cash.

When was the last time that you looked at establishing terms with vendors that demand prepayment or asked for term extensions or even early payment discounts?

And, even in a credit card society, many small businesses still rely solely on checks where others have learned to maximize the benefits of a charge card. When a vendor who provides 30-day terms is paid with a credit card on the 30th day, the credit card can have up to 30 days itself before its statement closing date. A month after that, the real bill needs to actually be paid. So, what was once a 30 day term can now be stretched to up to 90 days. Paying the credit card on time and in full generates no interest expense, and, as a bonus stacks up frequent flyer miles for the next airline trip. Almost all office expenses, including utilities, health insurance, and supplies, can now be paid on an office credit card.

To some, this may be business as usual, but, considering the cost of late fees, interest, and penalties, if utilizing the benefits of a credit card—even one where the balance is paid in full every month—isn't in your game plan, it should be. On another note, there is no one better to fight the fight on your behalf against a bad product or incomplete service than the credit card company. You usually just need to file a claim and, if there is no remedy, await your credit.

Within an accounting staff, a senior bookkeeper will realize that paying an insurance in full (when an agent can extend quarterly terms) or asking for term adjustments that are contrary to invoice demands, should be routine parts of a normal business process. Similarly, asking for overpaid taxes to be returned and not applied to next year's tax bill or demanding that a vendor's credit be given in cash instead of held for a future purchase take sharp, attention-to-detail skills that senior experienced staff have learned over time.

Likewise, a senior purchasing agent will not order goods today that are not to be used for several months. And, if something needs to be returned, it needs to be returned, not stacked in a corner and ignored. Just-in-time, just-enough ordering and just-in-time, just-enough paying will keep as much cash in hand as possible but needs real-time information, along with experienced management, in order to succeed.

The trick here is to value the cash that has been collected, never paying out more or less than is needed and utilizing appropriate credit to protect cash flow.

Knowing Your Budget

"Every business owner knows the monthly budget and lives within the company's means." Well, if only this were the truth, red ink would not exist.

If ever there was a case for utilizing senior people with senior skills, hiring a full or part time bookkeeper or controller in a small to mid-sized company is it. Even when using a high-end computer system, it takes experience and skill to manage an accurate budget, maintain budget to actual numbers, and deliver Profit and Loss statements, including accruals and depreciation, on almost a real-time basis. And this is exactly what is needed in a competitive, ever-changing service business environment.

Only with the knowledge that these accurate and up-to-date numbers can provide, does the struggling bottom line have the best chance to be a healthy positive value.

So, what is so elusive about having a budget? Isn't it just a matter of listing all the anticipated sales and expenses that a business can have? Well, yes, but it is fluid and a proper expense division between the cost of sales, which can vary, and the overhead costs, which are fairly fixed, is essential in managing cash flow, as well as boosting the net profit.

Here are a few of the standard areas of understanding and misunderstanding that need to be grasped when dealing with budgets.

Including All Possible Income

For a service business, without relationship sales accounts, projected sales income is usually some percentage above or below last year's sales numbers for various economic, strategic, or demographical reasons. If new markets are being entered or new products are being offered, a best guess at the resulting sales dollars will be added to the last year's sales figure. In addition, if there are heavy marketing efforts that will repeat past sales successes, more added revenue will be projected in the sales budget.

When retainer support plans, maintenance contracts, or any other yearly or monthly scheduled fees are added to the sales mix, however, a whole new dimension can be added to the budget. No longer are you solely basing sales projections on what you hope will happen, but, rather, you are looking at a portfolio of renewable contracts between your business and your client base. You then have not only the opportunity to increase sales if you enter new markets or invest in heavy marketing, but you also have opportunities to increase the value of your existing retainer plans, as well as engage your maintenance contract clients in expanded coverage.

For example, a consulting practice may offer a few different retainer plans, such as Plan A for $1,000 including 10 hours of labor at $100 per hour or Plan B for $3,000 including 40 hours of labor at $75 per hour. You can make a concerted effort in your new sales budget to convert a certain number of your Plan

A $1,000 spenders into Plan B $3,000 spenders. Yes, your hourly rate will be decreased, but there is much more to consider. First of all, your client will be given a "great deal" where their new $3,000 plan will provide 10 more "free" labor hours than three separate $1,000 plans would have provided. Secondly, with a larger contract in place, the client may tend to utilize more of your services, and, thus, you will keep your employees more fully booked.

Similarly, if you offer a "silver" maintenance contract for your air-conditioning service where you check the system once a year, you may budget to convert a certain number of customers to your higher-priced "gold" contract, where two visits a year are scheduled. If you offer one-year subscription services of any kind, you can budget to turn a certain percentage of your price-conscious clients into two-year subscribers.

With a client base that doesn't consist solely of one-time buyers, you have a much more predictable source for your budgeted sales. This book of business already has a value based on known contract numbers, and adding projected contract enhancements is a more respected calculated estimate than pure wishful thinking.

In any case, projected sales will have a more concrete, predictable foundation when the source of much of the planned new sales is based on existing contract holders.

The trick is to tweak and micromanage sales projections as much as possible using planned increases to existing client contracts, as well as projected sales to new customers.

Including All Known Expenses

By attempting to segregate expenses into three categories—fixed, sales dependent, and discretionary—we can get our arms around what is controllable and what is not controllable. A service business owner can then, at least, target covering fixed expenses on a month-to-month basis and have a much more immediate knowledge of where the bottom line rests. Even though some so-called fixed expenses (such as salaries) will fluctuate depending on sales volume, once the covering of fixed expenses creates the same sense of urgency as meeting payroll, the expense adjustments relative to the changes in sales volume will feel more intuitive.

The following are the three categories with a list of expenses that most services businesses have:

1. Expenses that are fixed:
   - Office expense, such as rent, mortgage, real estate tax, cleaning, maintenance, and repair fees
   - Utilities, telephone, telecommunication, and security expense
   - Equipment, supplies, postage, freight, and minor miscellaneous costs
   - Loans, interest, penalties, and bank charges
   - Insurance, accounting, consulting, and legal fees
   - Recruiting, training, dues, subscription, certification, and licensing fees
   - Auto expense
   - Salaries, outsourced labor, commissions, payroll tax, payroll fees
   - Marketing, such as direct mail, ads, telemarketing, and Internet forums
   - Income taxes
2. Expenses dependent on sales:
   - Products or expenses included in a sale
   - Outsourced services or labor included in a sale
   - Presale expenses such as auto, travel, and entertainment
   - Credit card expense if payment is charged
3. Expenses that are discretionary:
   - Bonuses and accompanying taxes
   - Owner benefits
   - Entertainment
   - Gifts
   - Donations
   - Conferences

With a solid knowledge of the current net profit along with a justified budget depicting future net profit expectations, an owner can more adequately make the snap decisions needed to stay in business, manage cash flow, and reap the profit that was expected.

The trick is to maintain real time records—orders, purchases, payments, receipts—all processed immediately and compared to up-to-date budget data. If sales have slipped, some planned expenses will slip and if sales have increased, some expenses will increase. Knowing which expenses are sales dependent and which expenses are fixed, with more stringent cash flow requirements, will help avoid large, potentially deadly surprises.

Working to the Bottom Line

Budgets are a must; real-time accounting data is a must. But, for a service business the essence of profit and ensuing cash flow comes from two sets of data:

1. Job Costing
2. Time and Billing

Everything about pricing a job or a product to be sold, including adding up costs of goods, labor, and overhead makes up Job Costing.

Everything about time spent by service providers, including all project- and non-project-related time makes up Time and Billing.

Together these two systems can make or break a service business. Here is the crux of the value of each.

Job Costing

When construction contractors need to price new jobs, they go to the jobsite, walk around with a pad, take some measurements, and return to the office to price it out. They then obtain material costs from the lumberyard, reach out for any subcontractor costs, and then guesstimate the amount of labor hours that will be needed to get the job finished. When all of this is done, an overhead number is thrown on the quote and the customer is given a proposal.

This model is familiar to everyone, but for many a service business, sometimes this whole function is actually skipped. Whether the service business includes goods or does not, a job is a job and an hour is an hour. A price needs to be competitive, but it also needs validation. What will it actually cost to do this work?

Computer systems are ideal to automate Job Costing. Because of the speed with which prices can be developed, an automated Job Costing system will save the owner from mistakes, misjudgments, and the pure laziness that happens when the tediousness of verifying what are sometimes small numbers, does not seem worth the effort.

First, there is a job, a service, a product, or a mix of all these things. We need a price—something that the customer will be willing to pay.

We need to look at what this customer or other customers have paid in the past for this or something similar to this.

We need to have all of the required cost components—the amount of in-house labor needed, the cost of that labor, the goods that we need to buy, any outside labor that is needed, any auto or other job-related expenses—and then we need "competitive costs." We need to check here what we have paid for goods or outside labor in the past; we need to verify that these numbers are still valid and competitive. Adding all of these costs of the job together, we are left with adding an overhead figure. This is where our budget must be as perfect as possible. When all these pieces finally add up to a price, we still need to check that the price is actually competitive in the marketplace.

Voila! We have done the budget part of the Job Cost, and, hopefully, we can sell the job, service, product, or combination thereof.

Once sold, again we hop on the treadmill. We need to record the real costs of doing the job, verifying that we were correct in our budgeting and actually made the money we expected to make. Any vendor costs or outside labor costs that were anticipated in the sold job should have been used to create purchase orders and should, thus, be later compared to the received Accounts Payable invoice. Any related expenses, such as entertainment, auto, and gas, need to be properly allocated and compared to the budget. Likewise, the actual labor hours are recorded as the work is performed and these hours need to be compared to the labor we had estimated in our budgeted Job Cost.

Knowing the budgeted versus actual Job Cost information is invaluable and goes a long way toward keeping the company profitable and keeping cash flowing. Doing all of these functions by hand, however, is prohibitive.

There are shortcuts that can be employed and, certainly, something is better than nothing. For instance, just estimating hard costs and inside labor estimates on something to be sold can be one avenue. You can then apply whatever cost markups are competitive for the goods portion and whatever market labor rate you have established for your labor portion. Comparing the actual costs that come in and the actual labor time that is used against the budgeted costs and budgeted labor in the job will point out any errors for the next price quote. With this method, you do not budget for overhead in the Job Cost. Instead, you simply use a Gross Profit (the price the customer pays less the cost of any hard goods or outside labor) as a bucket and measure the accumulated Gross Profit against all of your company-wide fixed and discretionary expenses. In other words, whatever money you earn that you do not have to pay to job-related outside vendors must be enough to pay all of your fixed and discretionary expenses.

The trick, of course, is to bring in more money than you have to pay out, period. Job Costing allows you to know that you actually made money on each job and product that you sold. So, when there is a problem with missing profit or when the absence of cash just does not make sense, we have all of the information that we need to find the culprit right at hand.

Time and Billing

Just as everyone is familiar with the construction contractor estimating a job with a pad, pencil, and tape measure, everyone is pretty familiar with a lawyer or accountant charging by the hour for the work they perform. Whether the service business, indeed, charges by the hour or whether there are a series of fixed prices that represent hours of work, service is labor and a service business either uses human labor or resells utility functions that require managerial labor.

In any case, for all employees who are service providers and who are paid because they produce products or services that are sold to clients, it is vital to the bottom line to know what they do with their time.

Lawyers will spend their days working on different client cases; a lawn care provider will go from house to house; a physical therapist will move from patient to patient; and a repair person will move from broken item to broken item.

So, how many hours does the service provider bill to customers throughout the day? How many hours are down-time hours or nonproductive hours? What is the correlation between the hours that are billed to clients and the salary that is paid to the employee? These are the questions that are answered when Time and Billing is added to a business's record-keeping functions.

If profits are to be made in a service business and if income is to cover expenses, then it is extremely important to utilize service providers in a cost-effective manner.

Looking first at a situation in good times, for instance, a full time, 40-hour-per-week employee may normally have 30 billable hours of work to perform in a week for the clientele. This employee might earn $1,000 per week or $52,000 per year and have additional benefit and tax costs bringing the total expense of employing this person to an actual $72,000 per year. This same employee may bill clients only for 46 weeks per year, counting time off for vacation, personal days, and holidays. So, if clients are billed for 30 hours per week at $100 per hour for whatever service is being performed, the income to the business is $138,000 (30 hours per week at $100/hour for 46 working weeks). So, the employee costs the business $72,000 and the business earns $138,000.

Now, maybe times are bad. The same employee does not have enough work to do or, worse yet, has the work but does not do it. Either way, this same employee is now billing clients only 20 hours per week, employed for the same 40 hours, and costing the same $72,000 to the business. Now the business is only earning $92,000 (20 hours per week at $100/hour for 46 working weeks). In a snap, without watching the store, the business' profit went right down the drain, losing $46,000 (the original $138,000 in billing 30 hours to clients versus the $92,000 in billing 20 hours to clients). Now, for an office of 10 billing employees, losing this kind of planned income will break the bank.

Hence, an accurate Time and Billing system must be implemented. Whether we are measuring the number of lawns mowed in a day, the amount of time actually billed to client jobs, or the patients seen in a day, in a service business, time is money. An owner needs to have all of the information that is available that will contribute to the cash flow of the business, and, ultimately, the bottom line.

Of course, again, the tediousness of gathering and managing this information is eliminated with computerization, but even manual record keeping is better than no record keeping. Time needs to be equated to jobs performed so that the real value of the time is costed properly in the item or service being sold.

The trick here is to have a marketable price for the service or good and use the correct product and labor costs, not the perceived costs, when weighing profitability.

In Summary

As difficult as it is to watch a service business suffer with continual cash flow problems, it is that much more difficult to convince an owner that there is a light at the end of the tunnel if a tougher, sounder business approach to the sales process is taken. The "who is really in charge here" question often has "the client" as the answer. Unfortunately, this is akin to having teenagers establish rules for their parents to follow instead of vice versa, and, basically, needs to be stopped.

A client's demands should be for excellent service and not, necessarily, for the prices and payment arrangements that they think are appropriate. A business owner alone must establish what can or can't be handled with payment terms, price points, as well as cash flow. Yes, you need to be lean and mean, and yes you need to be competitive. However, if payment methods and sales strategies are not favorable to profit and cash flow, and, if the business wants to have longevity, then changes must be made.

Sales and management tactics to keep cash flowing can include:

- Packaging services and labor into prepaid retainer plan bundles
- Creating a maintenance contract business to cover proactive- as well as reactive-based service offerings
- Working with recurring fee schedules to fill in low-cash-flow time periods
- Managing the scheduling of work around collections
- Incorporating vendor-related income and expense into the cash flow calendar
- Planning for better credit management

Managing a better budget can include:

- Tightening up projected sales numbers
- Properly tracking expenses as fixed, sales dependent, or discretionary

Homing in on profit can include:

- Real time management of profit and loss on every job performed
- Managing labor allocation to properly establish costs

With basically the same service business in place, repackaging of sales offerings into retainers, maintenance contracts, and fee plans can go a long way to ending some of a business's lifelong battles with cash flow. More real-time budget versus actual numbers, properly priced jobs, and labor utilization will, all together, combine to eliminate the emphasis on chasing yesterday's dollars, allowing for more emphasis to be placed on selling and profit making.

Streamlining Management Costs

Goals
• Change the back-office focus • Manage for profit

Changing the Back-Office Focus

If expenses are kept in line for costs of goods, the office, and the workforce, and all opportune streamlining such as computerizing, outsourcing, standardizing, and revamping is done, then the back office is ready to be utilized as a more data-rich, interactive part of the business. A computer system can take over mundane, boring tasks, and then part- or full-time managers, along with accounting and administrative staff, can join forces with the company's service providers to create a more modern, interesting, profitable, sales-driven company model.

With every person having varying levels of management responsibilities, even the lowest person on the totem pole should be able to measure their contributions to the ultimate success of a new, more exciting company structure.

Here are some of the more up-to-date methods that the back office can use to be profit conscious and assist in revenue creation instead of representing the "necessary expense" image left over from yesteryear.

Accurate Information for Ultimate Value

The goal in today's service business is for everyone to own their job and own the responsibilities of accuracy and excellence that come with it. With information so visible, it is important that all company data be kept in accurate, real-time mode in order to facilitate fast, reliable service as well as the profits needed to sustain every employee's job.

So, wasn't this always the case? Wasn't a company's record keeping and information gathering always intended to be accurate? Well, yes and no. No longer is batch updating or batch researching of information on a weekly or monthly basis good enough to compete effectively. Just as personal lives have become governed by the immediacy of cell phones and email, so too, business requirements must be handled with a higher sense of urgency. It is a different process model when the goal is day-to-day accuracy and completeness instead of half

71

of a picture today and another half tomorrow. It's the whole picture that is needed—an up-to-date total view, as quickly as possible.

There are three categories where maintaining the most immediate, accurate, complete information will create the most value.

First and foremost, you need to have proper administrative and financial information. Among employee, customer, vendor, budget, prospective sales, and accounting information, no one set of data out trumps another in terms of the need for day-to-day updating and relevant importance.

Keeping the following sets of information current should hold top priority in data entry and administrative schedules:

- For employee information, maintaining proper names, addresses, business cell, business email, home, personal cell, and personal email data is crucial for quick day-to-day interaction, as well as emergency contact. Maintaining the status of business credentials, open work lists, and timely entering of job-related labor and expenses into the Time and Billing records will feed into customer, budget, job cost, and accounting systems, guaranteeing those systems' accuracy.

- For clients and vendors, access to all contact names, titles, business and cell phone numbers, email addresses, and website addresses have to be as up to date as possible. Having instant access to historical as well as current pricing, proposals, sales or purchases, projects, as well as any diaried notes can make the difference between poor service and great service.

- For budgets, the reason to have them is to use them. All expected administrative and job-related expenses, continually tweaked and accessible for purchase order and payable comparison, will save money and avoid potential costly or embarrassing mistakes. On the income side, budgeted sales for recurring retainer plans, maintenance contracts, or ongoing fees will not only be used to point out deviations from actual Accounts Receivable numbers, but will be used to generate renewal and sales lists.

- For sales leads, the Customer Relationship Management (CRM) system needs to be maintained on a daily basis with all prospective new client sales, as well as any potential sales to existing clients. Respecting and adhering to the time sensitivity of this sales data allows an owner, and all income generators, to keep a business finger on the pulse of future sales.

- For accounting information (including payroll, purchase orders, sales orders, Accounts Receivable invoices, Accounts Payable invoices, cash receipts, and payments) some data needs to be updated and some data almost updates itself. Job Cost information, for instance, may start as a quotation and once the job is "sold" can feed directly into sales and purchase orders, which in turn can feed directly into Accounts Receivable and Accounts Payable, which in turn move directly to the General Ledger.

With just these entries maintained on a current basis, the essence of profit and loss, sales projections, cash flow, job-by-job profitability, and employee time utilization are only a computer query away. And, with only a handful of journal entries for things like depreciation and accruals, a more accurate net profit and an up-to-date budget to actual analysis can be, at the least, part of a monthly review.

Just as important, your employees need the most up-to-date tools and information to work efficiently and to satisfy your customers. Building upon the office manual—the procedures in place for performing client work and the standards established for handling client problems—the following information should always be updated as quickly as possible:

- Tech support resources for phones, blackberries, laptops, and other business hardware and software
- Employee requirements for new certifications and accreditations

- Vendor product, support, and training updates
- Updates on office procedures or policies
- Updated company literature and sales information

With up-to-date information in hand, an employee can support and service a client without having to call the office or search the Internet for information. This information can and should be on-hand in advance.

And finally, you can't live in a vacuum; you need to spread an accurate message about your company, through marketing, as often as possible. The following are the most common, day-to-day marketing efforts that need to be tackled sooner rather than later:

- Clean up references to exemployees (such as in voice mail and email)
- Set up new employees with business cards, voice mail, and email
- Update time-sensitive information on the company website
- Update new product or service information on the company website
- Train new employees about your company—who you service, what you sell, and the other employees who work for you
- Notify clients of pertinent, impending business, or sales events

It's not that most of these functions are not performed; it's not that most of this information is not updated. The essence of change here is the immediacy and the completeness of the actions. One half of an accounting system does not tell the whole story; having several employees scramble for the same tech support information is a waste of precious time.

So, what can a business expect to gain by investing its manpower in immediate updating of information? The following are some Monday-morning queries that can be asked and answered accurately and in a snap only when complete, synchronized data has been maintained:

- How many billable hours or billable dollars of work has each service provider had for each week this month? Compared to last month? Compared to last year?
- What is the percent of employee utilization—are employees spending 80% of their work week servicing clients? 50% of their week servicing clients? Is this number going down? Staying the same? Going up? Should you shrink the workforce? Increase it?
- How much money did a certain client spend so far this year? How much did they pay for each of their goods or services? What profit (or loss) was made on every one of those sales?
- How do you stand at this minute with your budget versus actual numbers for expenses and sales?
- What open purchase orders do you have and when do you need to place those orders?
- What sales are projected for the rest of this year? By client; by product; by service; by profit margin? How does this deviate from your budget?
- Where have your new customer leads come from this month? Last month? Last year? Should you increase your exposure in the marketing areas that have generated the most new client interest?
- What is the current profit or loss, including all journal entries?
- Which clients are running low on their retainer plans and will need replacement plans; which clients have maintenance contracts needing upgrades or renewals?
- Which clients have not been heard from in the last few months?
- What cash is due into the business based on the workload of the next two weeks? The next two months?

You need to know that answers to important questions like these are valid and represent the data entry of all required components.

The trick is to be so proactive, accurate, and complete that time is saved, money is saved, and great value is added, in the information system that the company maintains.

Guarding the Bottom Line

With new opportunities for business growth, there are also new opportunities for business losses. As the back office makes sure that every expense is inspected and every sale's profit is analyzed, so, too, should every in-house and outsourced process be verified and managed with the tightest control.

For outsourced processes, such as software updating, security monitoring, offsite backups, hardware remote management, email hosting, website hosting, and Internet service, there is no such thing as assuming everything is being handled properly. First of all, someone in-house needs to be a point person, verifying that proper services are being performed and, secondly, the point person must make sure that extra, costly repair and upgrade services are not being automatically performed without a stamp of approval. Outsourcing and prepaying are not an excuse for overcharging or underperforming.

Another possible outside offender, needing tight management, is the Internet advertising arena where what seems at first glance to be the smallest of fees can quickly turn into hundreds or thousands of dollars without any return on your investment. You want your ads to appear in the right forums, not in gimmicky "just generate more of a fee" forums. You are looking to connect and if you do connect, the click on your ad or website is worth the price. If you are not savvy enough to prejudge your costs up front, then be cognizant of available online usage and cost reporting, which is usually pretty up-to-the minute. You can watch the use of your advertising dollars as it happens, tweak where necessary, and revamp visibility if it is not cost effective.

Using online recruiting sites is another area that needs tight in-house management and control. What could be easier than posting your open position online and then sitting back and waiting for perfect resumes to appear? Better yet, how easy is it to search resumes that are already posted by job seekers, finding a dozen candidates and choosing one with the most perfect fit? The problem is that the $595 or $995 fee does not usually allow for the time needed to wade through the posted resumes or to sift through the responses to your ad. Finding the right candidates, connecting with them, and interviewing them takes time. So, as your contracted recruiting time quickly runs out, your fee can double and triple before you finish your hiring process. You can implement planning and speed up the process to address this potential pitfall.

With in-house processes, in addition to managing timely accurate work performance, there are several areas where a watchful eye and ongoing senior management can save a company unintended costs.

If an employee's job is purchasing, vendor relations, or anything involving spending company money, purchase orders, competitive pricing, and proper recording of well-negotiated terms must be overseen. Every rebate, commission, or co-op program, likewise, cannot and must not get lost in the shuffle.

With client contracts, credit card authorizations, and any other signed documents, sloppy internal filing processes can be costly down the road, for example, if you need to produce a signed verification of a credit card charge. Client retainer plans and ongoing maintenance contracts, renewals, upgrades, and payments need tight, accurate management. For example, letting a client's hardware service contract lapse or not processing an insurance plan renewal could prove to be a very costly, sometimes business-fatal, mistake.

Unfortunately, managing employees in this high tech-age has also become more complicated. Whether employees can or cannot use business systems for personal use needs a firm, enforced policy. At the same time, employees can cause all kinds of trouble by even improperly handling the systems they are permitted, without question, to use. Accidentally sending unacceptable emails, sharing another client's secure information by mistake, children activating a client's program when playing on their parents laptops—all innocent, yet, sloppy mistakes that security and tighter in-house controls can prevent. Further, a disgruntled or misguided employee can wreak havoc on an office if the gates are not locked—hacking into emails, company data, and client data, and engaging in inappropriate, damage-causing Internet behavior. Security needs to be part of an office environment and all of the "locks" need to be as strong or stronger than the locks on the outside of the office building.

In a multitasking, high-paced, competitive, business environment, it might seem impossible to get everything done and manage what others are doing.

The trick is to take the time to understand every process and then to put the tightest, most appropriate, automated management policies in place, safeguarding the business and guarding the bottom line.

Information Sharing

Whether you update all company-wide information on time or not, if you do not have an easy, foolproof method to share the information among your office staff, the job might as well not be done.

Here are the most common sharing techniques for small to mid-sized service businesses.

First of all, the office network ties all PCs and laptops together either with cabling or wirelessly, providing a centralized location for all office financial and administrative systems. Of course, most offices have networked computer systems and, with hardware and all infrastructure costs certainly less expensive than they were in the past, this is a must for all businesses employing at least two people. However, the network, as well as the application software used to run the business, must be organized properly for one-time-only data entry, which results in timely and accurate ongoing data sharing. The days of the sales-person returning to the office to search through the file cab-inet for contracts or the technician needing to physically leaf through the maintenance manual to perform a repair are long gone. The valuable information now must be easily sharable.

The following are a few of the data sets that most small to mid-sized businesses organize on the network in employee-accessed locations:

- Company-wide information such as employee manuals, personal contact information, office procedures, benefit packages, tech support information for all equipment, client work procedures, client follow-up procedures, client problem resolution procedures, office scheduling, and data entry areas for Time and Billing, Job Cost, accounting, and sales.
- Client-specific information such as client history, contact information, previous sales, pricing and accounting in-formation, proposal and contract information, as well as job-related information.
- Vendor-specific information such as vendor history, prod-uct information, previous purchases, costs, tech support, and training information.

The inexpensive scanner enables hardcopy data to be scanned once and safely stored and shared. Joining an orga-nized network, organized processes, easy one-time entry, and convenient storage will result in optimum use by all appropri-ate people.

After storing all data in easily accessible network locations, remote access to the office system is the next step. The office network must be a tool for employees to use day and night and, to be effective, must be accessible from afar. Part of the dedication to maintaining accurate information also requires flexibility in how and when information is updated. Remote ac-cess to the office system not only allows the service provider on a job site to enter and access client information but it enables the parent, home with a sick child, to still perform an excellent job, entering and keeping system information accurate and up-to-date.

With laptops, personal computers, and Internet access becoming the norm at every home and office, the owner's only requirement for opening up the office network for employee remote access is to install the proper tools and establish a stringent security system.

In addition to remote access to a company's internal computer system, much of the sharing of information between employees is shifting to the Internet, where information needed for constant sharing is stored online instead of on the machine in the office.

While many owners of small to mid-sized businesses still feel warmer and cozier keeping their private information on their own office hardware, there is a growing list of business applications that run entirely over the Internet and that are gaining consumer confidence and, thus, market share.

Accounting done over the Internet (on hosted websites) is certainly available but hasn't, yet, topped the sales charts. However, there are Customer Relationship Management (CRM) systems for small and mid-sized companies, where sales prospects are loaded and managed online, viewable and updatable by world-traveling salespeople, that are very secure and user-friendly.

Certainly, most people are familiar and comfortable with hosting their website out of the office instead of setting up a separate hosting solution in-house. As the website is generally considered to house safe, nonsensitive information, consumers aren't as fearful as, say, putting their company's accounting information "out there." But the company website use can be stretched, allowing employees to password-protect information that is nonsensitive but internal to the company or client specific. It is, after all, easier to access the company website than to remotely log in to the office network. There is a lot to be gained by having password-protected pages on the website where employee-required information, such as technical specifications, training material, links to vendor areas, and other job-enhancing material is easy to find and easy to use.

Another use of the Internet, housing email out of the office is so inexpensive and common now that outsourced hosted exchange systems are becoming the norm. Rather than managing the hardware and software in-house to capture emails, these hosted email accounts allow an office to set up Internet-based office sharing systems, such as shared contact information, shared calendars, and other community data that every employee needs to access. The trick here is to establish proper, safe sharing techniques so that the data that every employee needs to obtain can be both updated and accessed from near and afar.

So, with the newly profit-geared back office in place, data systems are updated simultaneously and immediately, expenses are scrutinized, and both in-house and outsourced business processes are established and tightly managed. All appropriate company-wide data is also made accessible for both updating and sharing. The back-office managers and administrators are, thus, now much more of a bottom line contributor than they were in the past.

Managing for Profit

With the streamlined back office now creating a platform for more productive, profitable client service, it is now possible to establish certain back office management tasks as client-billable events.

No matter how a service is paid for, often there is a team of people behind the scenes helping to perform the task at hand, even if only one face appears before a client. If work is performed on a specific client job, whether it is fixed-priced to the client or billed by the hour, then the labor should be counted in the cost of the job for proper client pricing.

Sometimes hidden management costs that are directly related to a project, job, or sale are the prime culprit for the misinformation in the job costing calculation, generating higher overhead costs and lower job-specific costs.

For instance, with up-to-date Job Cost and Time and Billing data in place, an accounting administrator may take on a project manager role, directing specific client job activities, providing management reports to clients, and performing job-related follow-up services. It may seem like a natural progression for a person with information in front of them to take on the role of a liaison, spending hours of time discussing job situations with the clients purely because the information is close at hand.

On the other end of the spectrum is the most senior service providing expert at the company. This person has provided excellent service to clients for years, knows almost everything there is to know, and is an invaluable resource to all other employees. Instead of working in the field or keeping a full, client-filled plate, this person fights fires all day long, saves the back of any employee having client-related difficulties, and saves the company from impending disasters time and time again.

Both of these people serve the company well but are their hours attributed to the work they are performing? When services are priced is the job costed to include the salaries of these two invaluable resources?

More times than not, the answer is no. So, this is a problem and a direct hit on the bottom line.

The following are some ways that small to mid-sized service businesses can create an income stream from the management costs that are directly attributable to a client service.

Fixed Pricing

When labor charges do not need to be broken out for a client's inspection, this does not mean that the appropriate labor shouldn't be posted and costed through a Time and Billing system to the proper job. The fixed-price job must create profit, and without the proper labor postings jobs will continue to be under-costed and under-priced. So, if a patient arrives for an appointment with a doctor and someone needs to first set up the examining room and then a nurse needs to check the patient's temperature and blood pressure, then these three people's labor needs to be calculated when establishing the cost of the office visit, not just the labor of the doctor.

Unfortunately, sometimes the costs we end up seeing are costs we don't want to see. How can we raise a fixed-price rate that is market-competitive and that the client has been paying for some time? Well, we can pretend that our costs are lower and see if that works, but if we are suffering with a disappearing bottom line, this is clearly not working. Perhaps trimming some other component of the fixed-price event, such as labor time allotted or products included will allow the price to remain the same. Or, maybe combining the incorrectly priced service with another higher-margined service will help the cause.

Many times weekly service providers will be very cost competitive with the labor that is charged, but will make up the profit selling high-margin supplies. Consultants, attorneys, accountants, and other professionals will "can" solutions so that the fee charged for a standard business analysis, estate plan, tax preparation, or other routine service will include enough of a previously developed, now lower-cost template to allow room for the remaining high-end expenses and still return a profit.

The trick here is to step up to the plate; know the true costs involved in the price you are charging for a service and make a business decision on how to cover the actual costs with facts in hand.

Hourly Billing

Although there are many professional service companies, such as attorneys and accountants, that bill clients for photocopying, secretarial help, and senior management review, there are also many industries where this blatant exposure of the components of a bill are unacceptable. True, these services have to be covered in a price somehow, but it is on a case-by-case, field-by-field basis as to whether it is competitive to present a bill broken out in this manner.

When working in an hourly billing environment, in trying to cover the cost of the two unseen and unbilled project workers, one the back-office accounting administrator performing client project management work and the other the senior support manager who fights every other support peer's fires at the office, there are three possible solutions:

1. You don't bill for the service that actually has been performed;
2. You do bill for the service that has been performed at your standard hourly rate; or
3. You bill in leveled rates so that the senior manager with infinite expertise has a higher rate and the junior accounting administrator, taking on a project manager role, is billed at a lower rate.

There is a compelling case for charging different rates for different levels of employees and it does make it more palatable when defending an invoice, based on hourly billing, to a client. For instance, the highest-priced employee who provided behind-the-scene help for a lower-priced employee may have billed only 30 minutes of their time. So, a client is actually saving money by not using this person for the whole task. Similarly, the accounting administrator, who is more of a project manager, has a lower rate and, therefore, provides more of a bargain than having a senior, more expensive employee perform the same task.

In any case, the labor has been performed and how it is billed to the client is an industry-by-industry matter.

What must be avoided is the problem where one billing rate exists for all levels (junior and senior) of employees. Depending on the type of service provided, this single-tiered billing rate can create a situation where the most senior employee is desired by all clients and the junior-level employees will be disappointing in comparison. Letting a client choose to work only with a senior partner for double the price can at least put the spending decision into the client's hands. You will, however, face a competitor's claim that their lower price covers senior and junior-level help. That kind of claim often requires the experience of disappointment to be effectively combated.

Another possible solution, which many consulting firms use to cover the project management by the accounting adminis-trator, as well as the fire-fighting done by the senior manager, is the management fee bucket. When retainer plans are sold or any kind of maintenance contract is sold, a flat fee is removed from these plans to cover management fees. So, if there are 10 hours of labor sold at $1,000, the actual invoice might be $1,100, or $1,070, or any amount to cover the management fee for the labor being provided. Although at first glance, this may seem like something that will cause clients to balk, it can be presented as a model where it saves the client money. When more expensive background managers post their labor hours to a client's bill, paying a one-time management fee, where all background help is forevermore included, can be presented to the client as a cost saver.

Ultimately, the issue with management costs is twofold. First, the price of labor to perform a service must be considered when pricing the job and, second, a decision has to be made whether to charge the client for actual work performed or to avoid the issue.

The trick is to make a profit and at the same time do an excellent job and please the client—it is not always easy.

In Summary

A service business model in the past may have had an office filled with high-, mid-, and low-level administrators, seemingly working for the business, but not working with clients, not assist-ing service providers who do work with clients, and not working to create profit in any way. In other words, the model was man-agement or back-office heavy.

As staffs shrink to compete in a leaner marketplace, more inside, back office work needs to be done by less people. And, the back-office also needs to be more than ever in collusion with employees who provide face-to-face or frontline client support.

After modernizing and streamlining a service business so that less people actually can get more work done, then it is time for a revised back office to really begin to contribute more to the bottom line.

Changing the back-office focus can include:

- Keeping all office data fully accurate, up to date, and synchronized
- Understanding and tightly managing all in-house and outsourced business processes
- Creating a user-friendly, accessible method for data updating and data sharing

Creating profit centers to cover management efforts can include:

- Knowing and including all costs of labor, including back-office labor, when creating fixed-price job prices
- Establishing tiered billing rates or management billing buckets to cover hourly billed back-office client-related labor

A data-rich, data-connected workforce can help elevate the service level provided to clients and at the same time contribute to the company bottom line. Watching every penny, eliminating waste, and managing for excellence are all higher level tasks that back-office management can address once automation and streamlining remove any leftover routines that might have been mired down in drudgery.

Finally, not only will it be in the business of saving money, but also the back office can participate in client management services that can result in generating real income.

CHAPTER

Raising the Marketing Bar

Goals

- Network
- Cover all bases
- Strategize

Networking

Not long ago, company networking conjured up a very specific image—suit-wearing men and women, "Hello" labels, cocktails, big smiles, and big hand shakes. Business card exchanges, association luncheons, and peer-honoring dinners allowed business owners to meet, greet, establish new contacts, and generate new sales. Although many of these business socials still exist, leaving one's office to attend business-to-business events, conferences, seminars, and, in general, to network, has increasingly become a faded memory. The following are some newer networking venues that many small to mid-sized businesses use to supplement or replace the fading face-to-face business forum.

Online Networks

Even a crystal ball could not have predicted how, within less than ten years, social and business online networking would reach such epic proportions with hundreds of millions of users. Social networking sites such as Facebook and MySpace along with business networking sites such as LinkedIn are increasingly used by companies and individuals to promote business. Where a collection of business cards served the purpose in the past, now friend, business, and peer connections on a network site come equipped not only with current contact information but a full and complete profile—job history, education, personal interests, pictures, recommendations, websites, associations, affiliations, and, most importantly, a long list of further networking connections. And, connecting with someone else's connections is surprisingly easy—common colleges, common friends, common professions, and common interests are all easy door openers, but blatant business-to-business contacting, recruiting, and referencing is quite the norm and quite acceptable.

Wikipedia, which describes itself as a collaborative encyclopedia, can also store historical, as well as current company and employee data. Because you can edit the information directly, it can be a venue for announcing new product and service information, and, in general, can house whatever promotional material a company wants to share with the universe of website readers.

Not to be ignored, YouTube is used not only to post laughing baby videos, but an increasingly wide variety of business materials, such as training videos, new product demonstrations, service presentations, reference snippets, company tours, and other pressworthy business messages.

And if you think there is no legitimate business use for Twitter, think again. There may not be a big demand for reading micro-blogs about finishing someone's income tax return but, if you are in the business of spreading information, providing real-time news, convention or meeting coverage, or up-to-the minute gossip of any kind, the small message blasts created using Twitter can be of value.

So, perking up the networking avenues is what it's all about—staying modern, going with the flow, finding the new standards in an ever-changing world of connections. You have a website; you link to your YouTube video; you profile yourself and your business on LinkedIn, Facebook, Wikipedia, and the new sites yet to come.

The trick is to stay on top of your game—to keep old, pertinent networking standards in place, but also to reach out for new opportunities, challenging you to learn and use the newest tools to grab and keep a newer market.

Blogs

Blogs are everywhere, and, for the skeptic, they can seem all-too self-promoting. However nonsubtle they may seem, they are, nonetheless, still message spreaders.

Luring an audience to read your blog is the goal, and, whether the blog is on the company website or it's a micro-blog created using Twitter, engaging readers and keeping them connected is the mission.

Most canned website tools come blog-equipped, or alternatively a separate blogging tool can be added to a current site.

So, what would a severe techno-phobic business owner do with a new blog? How could it possibly help a 20-year-old service business to gather a new audience?

Well, vendors, news bureaus, and employees all have a wealth of information that your customer may want to read in small doses. Recruiting an in-house blogger to spread some news might be a first step. And, connecting to a business-to-business customer is not always at the owner-to-owner relationship level. Employees at your customer's site may be Internet-savvy online addicts, working all day trying to accomplish anything and everything that doesn't require human contact. These same web-aholics may be just the people who are responsible for placing your orders and service calls or just, basically, maintaining a relationship with you.

So, a little article is written on the blog, comments are welcomed, and a link to the article is passed in an email to your clients: "New tax benefits for manufacturing firms," "Company A has been sold to Company B," "Ten employees finish the New York marathon."

Looking for examples? Want to see what other small business blogs are all about? A search on the Internet for "best business blogs" or "small business blogs" will provide plenty of examples to weed through. And, keeping your audience in mind will help direct the kind of writing that would be most appreciated by the members of your virtual network.

Most email/Internet users are familiar with the little snippets of information that constantly come their way throughout the day. The trick is to have short, sweet, enticing headlines and interesting enough content to:

- Keep a reader's interest.
- Guarantee a return visit.

News Columns

As many a business professional has learned, having your words in print establishes credibility and markets to the entire audience of the publication. We hear every day about the decline of the printed newspaper and magazine industry. With online news, however, whether generated by what was once a print-only bureau or by a newly created online-only venue readership is skyrocketing.

So, aren't these online news forums filled with so-called journalistic experts? Can the column about 401(k)s or estate planning, so welcomed in the past by the local press, get published online and, better yet, read? The answer is yes, yes, and more yes but, just like the information written in a blog—boring is boring. Short, tempting headlines are needed to lure a reader into actually clicking on and reading what you want them to read. Articles can also be enhanced with free or small-fee web-shared photos or videos, referenced through the news publication that you use.

Again, the articles that are newsworthy for your client base can be added to your website as a news stream, and, with the urgency of a press release, can be used as content in your email tag lines, articles in your company newsletter, and/or just as a basis for mass emails to your clients.

The online news publications leading the pack, such as Google, MSNBC, CNN, and AOL might not be where you want to go to start your news column. But, rising online-only newspapers in your area, as well as online versions of more regional newspapers, can be exactly your type of forum. Spending a half hour Googling your options can create a great lead list. Many smaller publications and start-ups are looking for experts of all kinds to share their knowledge and "fill the space." Often, small vertically-targeted online publications will find your articles and point their readership to them.

In addition, using a search engine to look for your name or your company name, once you have published your news online, will bring up a list of your articles, enhancing your exposure and your credibility.

What's interesting with both online blogs and news columns is that a young, savvy, otherwise low-level company employee can become completely engaged in the company's success by managing what is a natural, youthful pastime—Internet networking.

The trick is to make the commitment to this newer form of marketing—finding the publication, signing on as a contributor, connecting all the dots with your online portfolio (website, networking profiles, email connections), writing a newsworthy article, and then, finally, making sure that your customers, as well as potential customers, read it.

Web Conferencing

Without leaving your desk or without leaving your home, at any time, day or night, you need little more than a PC and a telephone to conduct a webinar—group meeting, sales presentation, or production demonstration.

Anything that you can do on your own PC can be done on a webinar for a group of people in lieu of a face-to-face meeting.

No more reserving hotel conference rooms, lunch reservations, and expensive audio/video equipment only to have only 3 out of the 30 registrants actually appear.

Web conferences can be routinely scheduled promotional events for a general audience, specially scheduled meetings for targeted groups, or just a one-to-one meeting where a presentation can be viewed interactively by each attendant.

The service that allows this type of web conferencing is usually free for a few tries and then very inexpensive to use on an ongoing basis.

Owners from another era may wonder what on earth their company could do on these types of conferences—just like their initial skepticism towards blogs, business network sites, mass emails, and online news columns. Isn't this just another technical gimmick that respectable buyers and owners will find objectionable? Isn't a face-to-face presentation, meeting, or demo always more professional and complete than anything that you log in to on the Internet?

Well, changing times make immediacy a major issue—people want to see what they want to see *now*, not next Thursday at 2 PM. Also, a global business community will allow demonstrators, service professionals, and meeting attendees to be located anywhere there is Internet access—even on different continents—to view and share the same information without the expense of an airline ticket or a hotel room.

So, web conferences can be arranged quickly, within minutes; they are inexpensive to conduct and save an enormous amount of money previously geared toward travel and meeting expense. People from all over the globe can communicate easily and examine business issues thoroughly. This sounds like a win-win situation. Well, it is!

Sales presentations, product demonstrations, training sessions, and collaborative work sessions are prime web conferencing candidates. Often, too, a salesperson will actually be face-to-face with a client, using a projector to enlarge the web conference presentation given by remote experts.

WebEx, GoToMeeting, and Microsoft Live Meeting are just a few of the web conferencing options that small to mid-sized businesses may use. Topics can be chosen, schedules can be created, and your message can be easily and systematically spread for an hour once a week on one of these conferences.

The trick is to learn the presentation skills needed for the most effective, fast, concise, quality web events. Contrary to face-to-face meetings, you cannot see what the attendees are doing. If your attendees are not totally engaged, it is far too easy for them to start reading and sending emails or even to take a nap rather than sit attentively through a slow-moving web conference.

Forums

Many a new start-up entrepreneur will spend endless hours on the Internet researching, blogging, exchanging ideas with other business owners, and networking in online forums. From college alumni sites to association, professional, and vendor sites, there are many small worlds where a budding business authority can gain an audience and a network.

If you are a computer consultant trying to troubleshoot a problem, many technical gurus will be happy to post their suggested remedies on various technical forums. Many large software vendors, such as SAP for instance, use forum-based support where vendor experts interact directly with users around the globe, joining forces to answer posted questions and solve technical problems.

News outlets and websites, purely in the business of forum sponsoring, will have organized online discussions on dozens of topics. Any topic from adoption to nutrition, to politics to local children's sports, can support a forum with a base of fans.

You can interact and pass your advice to people, local and afar, on almost any topic. And, it's not that difficult to develop a presence that is recognizable on various travel, restaurant, geographical, professional, or political sites. Now, if your business matches the forum that you frequent, you are establishing a network of business peers, referrals, and, even, clients.

Finding forums is, again, as easy as spending a half hour on Google, searching for your targeted area of interest, such as "nutrition forum" or "real estate forum" and checking it out.

The trick is to focus on your business goal, do the research that is needed to find a few forums, share your expertise, and always use your updated, professional online profile to establish your identity and credibility.

Webcasts and Podcasts

Updating profiles, blogging, publishing news articles, and writing in forums certainly spreads your written message, and the next level, managing a series of webcasts and podcasts, elevates your networking capabilities to a much more sophisticated, high-tech level.

With webcasting, an accounting firm can conduct credit-bearing certification sessions, a company's annual meeting can be viewed, or a vendor can unveil a new product. The webcast can be seen on-demand, but will typically be a live, scheduled event, broadcast over the Internet and requiring preregistration. There might be publicity involved and "buzz" that will encourage attendees to stop what they are doing and sit in on the broadcast.

Podcasts, on the other hand, are usually a prerecorded audio or video series. The podcasts can be automatically downloaded to subscribers using a web feed or can be downloaded on demand.

Like radio or television shows, your podcasts can be a series of business lectures, interviews, or discussions and can be listened to or viewed over and over again. To get some ideas on topics and formats, Google "business podcasts" or visit sites like iTunes. Checking out free podcasts will give you a lot of ideas.

Certainly, offering a schedule of webcasts and a series of downloadable podcasts can set you apart from the competition, especially the competition that isn't online.

The trick here is to expand your networking services, raising the bar on your offering with webcasts and podcasts and, thus, attracting more web-savvy clients.

Covering All Bases

Some small to mid-sized businesses do not even have a budget for marketing expense. It's not that new sales are not important to these companies; it's the marketing methods themselves that are restricted. Word of mouth and referrals sustain many a local service business, and, if that is good enough for success and longevity, then so be it. If business is slowing down, however, or profits are sinking as the business tries to maintain a long-established business model, then it's time to grab the reins and put a strong, stable marketing plan in place.

Marketing for small to mid-sized businesses does not have to be overly expensive. It does, however, need to be routine, ongoing, and systematic.

The following are some old and new marketing ideas that many service firms use to generate the business leads they need to sustain sales, maintain profits, and succeed in a competitive business landscape.

Laying the Groundwork

Traditionally, when a new service business opened its doors, there would be an immediate need for a marketing package consisting of a logo, business cards, letterhead, envelopes, and a company brochure. Of course, there would be an existing business address and a telephone number to use.

Fast forward to today, and a virtual company can exist without a business address at all as long as there is an email address, a cell phone number, and a website. Looking professional and experienced also used to be all about having expensively printed company hand-outs but this can now be had by any company, with self-publishing tools, a laser printer, and/or a visit to a local small business printing center. Custom-designed websites used to be cost-prohibitive for smaller businesses. Now, they can be sophisticated, cost effective, and dynamic using the newest low-cost developmental tools on the market.

So, today's new business starts out with addresses: web, email, and possibly office. Like yellow page ads and white page listings of the past, networking profiles of the company and key employees are set up on Internet registries and networking sites, such as LinkedIn, Wikipedia, and Facebook. The website is designed and developed, providing sales-driving product and service information, and marketing material that separates you from your competitors. And, rather than reinventing the wheel, white papers, service and product information to be used on the website and in printed company material are gathered and reprinted from vendors, professional affiliations, or syndicated sources. Business cards, brochures, and all printed company letterhead and forms can either be self-published or inexpensively outsourced to other experts.

Mentioning the marketing start-up tools for a new business is important because a long-standing business must also be on board with these base marketing components. Too often, there isn't an ongoing push to stay up to date. Employees may come and go, product and service information changes and, just as a new start-up company needs to present a face of experience and success, so does the business with longevity. A new client may be judging your long-standing business against a brand new start-up whose whole marketing image is fresh, impressive, and modern.

If you want to see if you measure up, start by trailing a few business peers through their online networks. See what they have on YouTube, LinkedIn, and Facebook. Check out their websites. Then look at the largest, national competitors that you can find in your field. How does your profile look in comparison?

The trick here is to go back to basics—get the groundwork in place as if you were starting a new business. If this means updating your literature, updating your web presence, and keeping an ongoing check on old outdated information that is floating around, then that is the task at hand. Make sure that the level of professionalism and experience that your company has is the image that you portray to the outside world.

Blatant Advertising

When it comes to service businesses, some services are more emergency driven than others. When a tooth aches, a pipe bursts, or a roof leaks, someone needs to be found as soon as possible to solve the problem. For other services, there is not the same sense of urgency and a buyer may act on impulse or take his or her time making a decision. In any event, a company needs to advertise itself in order to be found when needed or to have a reminder in place when a sense of immediacy does not exist.

Traditional print ads in newspapers, magazines, newsletters, and other publications are reminder types of ads where a little nudge is being given to take some sort of action. The bad news is that the printed-only media is losing readers and losing money; the good news is that, cost of advertising space aside, preparing the actual ads is usually easier and less costly nowadays using in-house software tools. Vendor co-op programs also sometimes provide ad layouts that, with only a logo and a personal

message inserted, can be used almost as is. So, including traditional print advertisements in your marketing plan may have a
lower readership level than it did in the past but will also have
less developmental costs.

Checking online registries and telephone directories or just
using search engines will usually suffice when an emergency
contact is needed, but for nudging customers into action, advertising on the Internet can either be a great or a not-so-great
idea.

Certainly, sophisticated professionals don't want to be ap-
pearing in an annoying pop-up window when someone is trying
to read a newspaper online. But well-placed links on complementary business sites are effective and nonoffensive. Vitamin
sites may link to nutritionists; furniture sites may link to deco-
rators; accounting software may link to CPAs. Wherever your
customers travel online, potential advertising opportunities
exist.

Search engines such as Google have ingeniously created an
auction type of direct advertising where your ad will appear
when a user enters certain search words.

Depending on the number of interested advertisers, you can
pay either a small amount of money for your ad to appear or a
large amount of money. Your fees will also rise or fall depending on whether anyone actually clicks on your ad. The other
interesting fact about this type of advertising is that your ad
can appear when there is a search on a competing business.
If you use your competitor, "Joe Smith Plumbing" as a target
of your advertising campaign, whenever someone searches on
"Joe Smith Plumbing," your competing business information
for "Bob Jones Plumbing" can appear as an ad on the screen.

Search engine optimization, which keeps a business at the
top of, for example, Google's result list, is certainly no small feat
to accomplish. With keywords, published press releases, videos,
blogs, news articles, and links to other sites all contributing to
a high search result, you can see that a lot of hard, continuous
work is needed to keep your presence not only known, but at
the head of the pack. There is a method to this optimization

madness, however, even if it does change by the minute, and diagnostic software, along with outsourced services, can help to identify and fix search weaknesses.

Direct mail and mailed newsletter campaigns have long been a marketing staple where x number of mailed items should expect y number of interested buyers. Vendors, associations, and other professional affiliates provide inexpensive, preformatted templates so that heavy development costs vanish and both direct mail and newsletter pieces can be quickly personalized and targeted for a customer base. The ongoing use of these mailers, however, has two problems. First, the business mailbox is increasingly becoming stuffed with junk mail and second, the cost of postage for a piece that might not even be read at all cannot compete with free email on the Internet.

Mass emailing services remove not only the cost of postage from the direct mail and newsletter transmission but they combine the actual document creation with readership and follow-up statistics. In other words, it is one-stop shopping—you provide a list of customers; you select a newsletter, mail piece, or you provide your own; the piece is emailed; reading habits are tracked and sales interests are forwarded.

Besides this type of advertising that is being directly passed in front of a potential customer, the spreading of your brand can also involve well situated name droppers on signs and promotional items. Whether it is a laptop bag, a business car, or the credit on a website, photograph, or brochure, your name is an important advertising element.

Lastly, both local radio and cable television have become more friendly to small to mid-sized businesses and testimonial advertising can be effective when nudging a potential buyer into making that call. Many businesses will target the drive-to-work crowd for radio exposure or the breakfast crowd for local cable exposure.

So, removing tired, expensive forms of blatant advertising like direct mail, and increasing new less costly Internet-based methods, and trying some tried-and-true brand spreading is a respectable plan for a small to mid-sized business.

The trick is to be modern and selective when you use direct advertising, measuring return on investment, and making any needed changes as fast as you can.

Subtle Message Spreaders

As opposed to the blatancy of an advertisement, a well-placed business article will have more of a newsworthy appeal and won't have that paid advertisement feel. The same can be said about news columns and blogs. The goal is to gain publicity for the company, the owner, or the employees, almost accidentally.

And with reporting about volunteer efforts, donations, or sponsorships, the feel good story is the focus of the article. Any mention of the business or the owner has to have a "by the way" feel and can't in any way appear to be self-serving.

The same can be said about membership in certain associations, clubs, or charitable organizations. Your good will and hard work for a noble cause is a complement to your strong work ethic and will also rub off on your business credibility.

Giving speeches, teaching classes, and serving as a resource for professional organizations are other ways to have your personal credits enhance your business reputation. Not only will you be able to tout your expertise and spread your knowledge to those seeking insight and improvement, but your credentials will become published in the event program, the agenda, or the school catalog. Without even attending your class, people will discover that you have expertise in their exact area of interest.

Other subtle message spreaders may seem accidental or lucky but are nothing of the kind. Just as working hard on search engine optimization will result in having your name pop up more often in online searches, so too, well-placed press releases will appear like news reports and won't reveal the hard work that was involved in the press release's placement.

Following your big website hit producers through Google Analytics will give you an idea of where you receive the most bang for your buck in your message-spreading plan. Links from articles, forums, news outlets, and direct searches will be measured, allowing successful methods to be duplicated.

The trick is to include these subtle message spreaders in your marketing plan. As every business owner knows, visibility, credibility, and reputation are vital to a service business's longevity.

Referrals

Most customer referrals are happily received and not solicited. However, there is a science to increasing referral business and it should have a place in a marketing plan.

First of all, all referrals are not the same. One person telling another person that they know a great painter is the typical type of referral, but, as it is with business networking, most successful plans are just that—plans.

There can be vendor referrals where you sell and service a certain product and the vendor refers service calls and new business calls to you. There are also referrals that your organizations and networks can provide. Sometimes these kinds of referrals take a little prodding. Maybe you ask a business peer to mention your sales training program in his or her monthly newsletter. You may, of course, provide a similar return courtesy in your newsletter.

Several service industries also have paid referral services where your certifications, experience, geographic and functional abilities are ranked and released to interested parties. These "brokers" sometimes receive payment from both the companies listing their products or services and the customers looking for a proper reference. Doctors, dentists, and many other professionals also receive referrals from agencies completely geared to connecting buyers and sellers of each service.

Searching the Internet for "referral businesses" in your field will alert you to opportunities that you may not know exist. If you are looking for a business software solution, for instance, you might go to "CPA online" or "find accounting software" where your needs are established and posted for software resellers to respond. "Find a florist" will refer you to a local flower shop.

Just thinking about referral methods used in different industries will help you find and develop your own referral base.

Finally, there's a practice becoming more and more common in professional circles—asking for referrals. It has become more of a common practice to ask a satisfied client for a reference letter and to specifically ask a client to refer you to others. Many vendors reward resellers of their products who have happy customer recommendations, and many businesses will publish their recommendations in company brochures or on the company website.

The trick is to respect the referral process as a marketing effort, to think outside of the box, and to explore referral opportunities that were dormant up till now.

Direct Contacts

So far, the marketing methods discussed have been preparatory —tools put in place, advertising plans established, good press for good deeds and referrals being set up. With just these efforts alone, new clients, new business, and greater profits can be expected. What's left to finish a marketing plan and to cover all bases are the actual face-to-face, person-to-person efforts that are needed to recruit possible customers and prepare to sell the products and services that the company has to offer.

Trade shows have two kinds of effects on a service business. First of all, a business may attend a trade show where there are new products, new services, and new solutions that can be offered to clients. At this trade show, the business owner is the customer, meeting new vendors, establishing new relationships, and coming home better equipped to service and sell to the company's customers.

The other effect of a trade show is where the business is selling its wares, its services, and/or its solutions to its own customers. At this trade show, the goal is to attract new sales prospects and return home with an arsenal of business cards and new leads. For some industries, large organized trade shows are the norm but for other industries smaller exhibitions such as Chamber of Commerce and vertical industry events present the same opportunities to meet and greet prospective new clients.

Similarly, a business may have a seminar, a presentation, or a conference—each is a venue where clients and prospective clients are invited to learn new things, perhaps buy new products, and sign up for new services that the business can provide. These meetings do not have to be in person and can be web conferences where audiences are wooed just as they would be in person. Software consultants will demonstrate new computer programs, accountants will present college or retirement plans, or investors will discuss portfolio management.

If not on the web, these seminars, presentations, and conferences don't necessarily need to be high-end, costly events. They can be equally effective when held in local libraries, bookstores, or at monthly state and local professional and trade meetings. Just as with subtle message spreading, opportunities for more direct sales presentations exist through continuing education programs at high schools, colleges, or even private adult education schools, such as The Learning Annex.

Telemarketing may be overexposed and certainly not welcome at dinner time but, nonetheless, especially on a business-to-business level, it is an expected form of marketing. Cold calling is a difficult task and not for the faint of heart but there is a measurable success rate and, in certain service industries, many new business sources are first uncovered through telemarketing.

And are there still door-to-door salespeople? There are. A salesperson's job is not only to service existing customers but also to meet new customers, visit new offices, and establish new contacts.

The trick is to incorporate face-to-face strategies in your marketing plan and face to face today can be in person as well as on the web.

Strategizing

Cost-cutting measures can usually provide instant gratification. Spending reductions have a dollar value and efforts are immediately realized.

Marketing efforts, however, are not always as easily measured. For a small to mid-sized business without a huge market research arm, what can be assessed must be assessed and what is subjectively measured will require the owner's expertise and judgment. Here are the basic elements of strategizing with regard to marketing efforts.

Starting at Ground Zero

If marketing efforts have never before been measured, there is probably some homework to be done. Do all customer records contain their original contact source—where you first met the customer? If they do, great; if they don't, either coding the records correctly or as unknown will at least start the ball rolling for future analysis. Are all historical customers and prospective customer leads even in a recorded system right now? They need to be. It is important that one of the big three software solutions for a service business's success be implemented and maintained with accuracy—the Customer Relationship Management (CRM) system. So every new or prospective customer, moving forward, will be recorded with a reference as to how you first met them. The sources will later be measured against marketing efforts, so categories such as referrals, telemarketing, direct mail, or seminars should reflect individual campaigns for proper analysis.

Next sales notes on prospective, new, and existing customers must be kept up to date. (Even if you have not done this in the past, you should make sure it is done moving forward.)

Finally, as part of the Customer Relationship Management's value, there has to be a direct link between the CRM information and the Accounts Receivable system. Sales to customers must be traceable back to the customer's original contact source as well as to the marketing campaign, if applicable, that brought the sale to fruition.

With all past and new client information coded and ready to go, a few other measuring tools need to be set up. If the service bureau used for mass emailing does not provide proper measuring tools, such as how many people actually read the email or how many articles in a newsletter were opened, then a better company needs to be hired. Along the same lines, some hosted website solutions offer site statistics showing website views and pages visited. If this is not available, Google Analytics provides a free service where website activity can be measured and analyzed. Outsourced telemarketers provide reporting tools with number of calls made and number of leads generated. If in-house telemarketers are used, the same inside reporting must be collected.

The most important measurement of marketing's success will result when 100% of all new prospective client or client records contain the source of the relationship. If you don't actually know the source, for instance, such as when someone calls into your office, you need to ask the question, "Where did you learn about our company?" Here's where some subjective interpretation will be used later on. If your blatant marketing and subtle marketing efforts are successful, a person may not even remember where they discovered you. They may say they saw you on a cable show that you weren't on or that they saw your ad in a magazine that you weren't in. This is good—it shows that your message is out there.

The trick here is to set up the measuring tools to measure what can actually be measured, leaving the questionable contact sources to be subjectively evaluated.

Measuring Your Efforts

There are three types of measurements that we try to do with our marketing efforts.

First, we want to see that strangers are paying attention to us. How many people have logged onto our website, where did they come from, and how long did they roam around on the site? Google Analytics or website activity reports can provide this answer.

If we used direct mail campaigns geared to strangers, did we have any responses?

When we send out mass emails, how many people read them? The email service bureau can provide this information.

So, step one is to determine how many strangers reacted to our campaign.

Second, we want to see how many strangers turn into sales prospects. We look at how many new leads we have entered into our Customer Relationship Management system and where these people originated. Were they at seminars? Did they see our ads or receive our direct mail pieces? Did they call our office? Ask for a quote? We can analyze how many of our leads came from which marketing programs and determine whether a program has been successful and should or should not be continued.

Third, we want to analyze our actual sales. For all sales, where did the customer actually come from? Were they originally from a seminar, sitting in our records for a year or two and now called to action with a mass email campaign? We want to analyze sales by original contact source, sales by individual marketing campaign, the cost of the marketing efforts versus the sales dollars realized, and our return on investment for every marketing effort for which we are engaged.

Going back to the judgment factor, we may realize that a certain campaign generated only one sales lead. With a cost of $10,000, this would not seem cost effective. However, the one sale may have a value of $100,000, which changes things a bit.

Similarly, a campaign may provide no sales leads but the cost is minimal. So, we may leave this in place, and analyze it again in the future.

It is pretty scientific to analyze the cost of a marketing effort versus the sales revenue attributed to that effort when all of our ducks are in a row and the information we have is solid. Sometimes all of the efforts—print ads, radio, television, and promotional products—are combined to deliver a new client. And, when we aren't 100% sure of where to attribute success, we are left with our gut feeling and, again, judgment.

Once we understand the numbers that we truly can rely on, we can have the confidence we need to develop marketing programs that are cognizant of seasons, cash flow slumps, holidays, and employee vacation periods. Second only to cash flow, marketing can have the biggest impact on a small to mid-sized business.

The trick is to be systematic and precise with the marketing programs, the measuring of results, and the strategizing moving forward.

In Summary

Just as cash flow problems will sink a small to mid-sized business, without a way to drive sales and attract customers, the best service business on earth will have no one to service.

With word-of-mouth and recommendations keeping customers coming, many businesses may not devote enough time and effort to formalizing a marketing plan. Should the sales base suddenly disappear or the profit margins for the existing client business drastically sink, what can be done to get a proper marketing program on track?

Developing strong networking avenues can include:

- Keeping old pertinent networks in place while moving into the online networking arenas
- Using business blogs to find a newer audience
- Writing an online news column
- Using web conferencing for presentations, demonstrations, training, and collaborative work sessions
- Finding and using forums to spread knowledge and "connect"
- Creating a webcast and podcast portfolio

In Summary

Covering all marketing bases can include:

- Going back to basics with business marketing start up tools
- Using cost-effective online and tried-and-true direct marketing programs
- Establishing subtle message spreaders to boost visibility and credibility
- Formalizing a referral base
- Marketing face to face at trade shows and online events

Strategizing can include:

- Setting up a Customer Relationship Management system with baseline customer source information
- Measuring marketing efforts and sales efforts for return on marketing investment

If developing a marketing plan is step one, consistently implementing the plan is step two. By far, the most important step, however, is step three—measuring results. With the advantage of a computerized office, knowing where the customers come from and the cost of getting their business can be measured and analyzed. Spending, thus, can be more targeted, marketing driven, and, finally sales based.

CHAPTER

Making Everyone
a Salesperson

Goals

- Enlist the troops
- Create a mantra

Enlisting the Troops

New to a fluctuating economic environment, new to this business generation, and perhaps new to the business owner is the fact that every employee needs full buy-in to the company that supplies his or her paycheck. Whether it is customer service, up-selling, repeat business, blogging, production, or accounting, there is an opportunity for all levels of workers to meld. For those just entering the workforce, for the technically skilled or unskilled, for the seasoned professional service providers, participating in procompany, sales generating behavior will add to the health of the business.

Here are some new ideas about remolding a service business into a profit-driving model where sales and profits are part of every person's job description.

Spreading the Message

From the telephone to email to face-to-face meetings, every employee has an opportunity to spread the company's message and engage in potential sales-generating behavior.

Starting with the telephone, taking messages and returning them is a given, but engaging a client or a potential client when they call the office, being aware of the full gamut of the company's sales offerings, relating to the client on a personal level, looking for up-selling opportunities and, in general, caring about the phone call is what really matters. No one wants to be passed from voice mailbox to voice mailbox. The client calling the office for anything at all should be treated with the same importance as the person that is funding the office payroll.

Email is a biggie. Starting with the signature line on every email and the tag line below, there is opportunity to promote the company website, add a company logo, emphasize the mission statement, link to a blog, or even offer a service. Adding a pertinent link to an email can be a great form of viral marketing, where you pass something to one customer, hoping that they will pass it to others, and so on and so on and so on. The body of an

113

email, also, can house reference links, videos, and researched material pertinent to a client's questions. So, treating email as a marketing tool should be an everyday event. And, emails to business peers, vendors, and nonclients are as important as any professional client correspondence. You never know where a new client is lurking. Misspelled, sloppy, noneffective emails reflect not only the employee but also the company that he or she works for. Take a survey and look at email signatures, website references, and any other tag lines on some of the emails that you have in your inbox. There are great ideas to be copied by checking out what is sitting right on your desk.

Face-to-face business meetings certainly have become less common but, nonetheless, in work, we still are what we wear. In a service business where someone is performing labor in front of a client, looking professional, wearing appropriate clothes and dressing for work and not the beach is not only a personal reflection but also a boost to the company's profile. And, even when face-to-face means web conferencing, being on time and attentive are other ways of stating that you respect the clients and respect their time.

Business networking was once solely the job of the company owner, the senior manager, or members of the sales staff, but now networking opportunities among employees at all levels at both customer and vendor firms is an everyday occurrence. With Facebook, MySpace, Twitter, and LinkedIn, online connections have blurred the line between personal and business lives.

On business network sites, just as with email taglines and website content, the profile that the employee presents is a direct reflection of their company. So, these new network avenues, visible and promoted at the office, further spread the message and interlock various levels of workers across client, prospective client, and vendor lives—purchasing agent to salesperson, receivables clerk to payables clerk. Networking is for all employees no matter what the job level!

While spreading the message for potential sales opportunities can, obviously, result in great value, spreading the word in-house, employee to employee, can also reap great benefits and reduce unnecessary losses.

Leading by example and just being a role model to fellow employees can help to create a company image that is a magnet for respectable new employees, as well as clients.

And with the Internet, so many workplace protocols are ignored that self-policing systems are more required than ever, and, far more effective than all the security systems a company can try to assemble. The trick is to make the honor systems clear and definitive.

For instance, with a busy daily schedule, customers waiting, and a backlog of work, would it be acceptable for an employee to go to the mall mid-afternoon, go out to see a movie, or call old college friends? Not at all! But Ebaying, YouTubing, and texting for hours doesn't seem to generate the same guilty conscience. And, if physically carting the company's financials home to share with friends over a beer is obviously wrong, why doesn't the copying of electronic company records and private documents generate the same criminal sense? Intra-office honesty and integrity must override a whole range of new bad habits, and the harm done by one "saboteur" can affect profits on the company's inside, as well as the company's reputation on the outside. Costly employee indiscretions certainly do not promote a more profitable workplace—they negatively affect everyone's bottom line.

The trick is to engage every employee in proactive message spreading and protectionism that will benefit the company outside the company walls as well as inside of them.

Breaking the Mold

Every office has the go-to person who can fix a printer, change the toner, or even open a jar.

It could be that the Senior Accounting Manager is a hardware guru or the receptionist fiddles with websites. In any case, buying into the company's sales success and profit generation can have new meaning, especially for an online generation.

Not only does caring about one's job "show" but interjecting one's hobbies or natural talents to benefit your workplace can lead to a company profit boost as well as a possible promotion.

Marketing is the most natural place where an employee's job description can be enhanced with a non-job-related trickle of something fun, yet extremely beneficial for the company.

Who knows about Facebook? Twitter? Who has a design flare to help update the company website or a journalistic itch to write a company blog or post news articles on the web?

Having an outside marketing firm work on placing news articles and press releases may be an acceptable budget line item, but learning about Google Ads, search engine optimization, and online news services may be best left to the in-house resident Internet geek. Corporate structures at marketing firms are just as rigid as they are at most other firms. Learning to utilize web conferencing, online forums, Customer Relationship Management software, and any other new marketing tools may be as much about learning on the job to the person at the firm you hire as to the person sitting at one of your own desks.

So, inside recruiting for anything and everything that will be a sales or profit generator needs to take place daily.

Take the person in charge of Human Resources who places ads on the Internet, using Monster or Craigslist. The first chore for that employee is to look for similar ads, see what job titles are utilized, the quantity of the ads, the differentiating qualities. Who is placing these ads? If you are an HVAC company, servicing and selling product X components, you will state that your new employee must have relevant experience using this product. Who else has a similar ad, for a similar employee, for a similar product?

Instead of finding just a competing service firm, you might find a potential client. For instance, a building management firm may be looking for the same employee that you are looking to hire. You may have just located a prospective client that needs to outsource some of their services, rather than continue to try to maintain service capabilities in-house.

So, the HR department can learn to be astute in locating potential sales opportunities. This is certainly now a common way online to find businesses that could use the services you provide. When employees think on behalf of their company, and see themselves as marketers and business advocates, all forms of natural entrepreneurial behaviors may evolve. And, if there isn't a natural blossoming, often a nudge here and there will evoke the same result.

What about the part-time receptionist, the college student working a few hours a day to pay the bills? In-house market research can shed light on all types of sales activities. Spending several hours looking at competing firms online, finding their offerings, their messages, obvious differences between their firm and yours, or spending several hours looking at your customers online, researching potential up-selling opportunities, or vertical market trends—the web provides a wealth of information that, perhaps, can be best browsed by Internet-savvy student types, regardless of their primary job description.

And what about good old idea generation by your existing employees? What do they see "in the field" when they work with your clients? What do your clients really want? How can this be converted to your sales and marketing efforts? What's wrong with what you are doing now? What can be improved? Do they see competitors with better answers?

Ask for ideas from people who aren't used to being involved at this level of proactivity; the results can be surprising. And, if face-to-face meetings with employees are not feasible, set up weekly web conferences. Mix things up. Have people deviate from their norm and think outside the box.

The trick is to break the mold of the rigid job description, and open the door for employees to be involved in sales and profit-generating actions and idea development.

Being Excellent

If a person's job is to perform for a client or to be in-house support to service personnel or to keep accurate company records for all to share and properly utilize, obviously only excellence should be expected. But what about each person's self-determination, search for growth, and personal career development? Before entering the workforce, many people will become accredited in their field, attend courses, graduate college, or, somehow, develop a trade. They create a resume that an employer will respect so that they can enter the job market. If there are requirements for the job, employees will develop new skill sets, possibly take additional courses, and pass mandatory exams. Many times, in small to mid-sized businesses, the only other developmental track on which a person will embark will be geared toward getting a new job one day with a new company. What's wrong with this picture? How can each employee do an excellent job and also remain competitive in his or her own job and within the marketplace? Personal growth, not mandated by a job description, can clearly be a boon to a company's gross sales and, ultimately, to the bottom line.

Certain fields, certain positions, certain career tracks demand and reward efforts above and beyond day-to-day job descriptions. Salespeople of every kind can be personally motivated to find new tactics, read self-help books, know their market, and grow to exceed the minimum demands of their job. A salesperson's salary is a big motivation here as sales commissions, many times, reward "out of the box" thinking and certainly more sales will result in a bigger paycheck. Accountants, attorneys, physicians, and many other professionals need to read journals, understand new law, and stay current on new research results, not only for the exact jobs that they perform but also for general knowledge and credence. Outside, mandatory licensing requirements also put demands on these professionals to obtain continuing education credits, which bring with them new knowledge and new exposure.

Helping to inspire and foster self-growth in all employees, whether for job-related reasons or not, is a boon to each person's self-image and to a company's overall personnel image. Reading daily newspapers, professional books, and journals enhances an individual's job marketability, and thus enhances a company's marketability.

To tickle the fancy of employees and to promote self-growth efforts that aren't job mandated, the tactics of large corporations can be copied and used, even in the smallest firms.

In-house newsletters, for instance, can be easily prepared with word-processing software and can be filled with course opportunities, recommended books, white papers, online learning tools, and certification paths. The same in-house newsletter can be a forum of praise for employee accomplishments and an introductory platform for employees to share newly accessed knowledge through articles and recommendations.

Roundtables, conferences, lunchtime meetings, and webinars can be used not only for outside sales efforts, but also for intra-office development, as well. An inquisitive, enthusiastically self-motivated workforce can have a dramatically positive impact on a service company's deliverables and reputation.

With employee-written in-house news columns, employee-run in-house webinars, and an atmosphere of self-improvement and shared-learning, employees are groomed for performing these same skills for sales-generating purposes on the outside of the company. Practice makes perfect, and knowledge-packed articles, welcomed in-house, can easily be converted to blogs, news articles, and client newsletters out-of-house.

And, just like their large corporate counterparts, small to mid-sized service businesses can utilize job titles and promotions that reward their employees when they seek continuing education. Client references, company profiles, and promotional literature can all be beneficiaries when employees work hard for their own self-development.

The trick here is to promote excellence not only in each person's specific job but in the areas of self-growth and self-development. For a service business, selling the image of a company is all about selling the image of the employees within the firm.

Creating a Mantra

When a service business has been in existence for any length of time, two things can be assumed:

1. There is a good service being performed
2. There is clientele

Too simplistic? Not really. You cannot create value in real estate without "location, location, location" and similarly, you won't find a successful nursery school in a retirement community or a booming lawn-care business amidst high-rise buildings. So, the ongoing entrepreneur has found a worthy service solution to sell and has located a matching clientele to use the service. This leaves only one problem—profit has to be involved.

You can lay out all the remaining puzzle pieces and start putting them in place, but don't overlook the biggest agent for a service business's turnaround, profitability, and longevity: an enthusiastic, great group of employees. A team of people marching to the same drum and singing the same tune can do more to create a profitable environment than any number of Google ads can do. The following are simple steps that a proactive, procompany employee base can do to help the cause and, in essence, help to sing the company's praise.

Knowing What's Working

Many times, in a service business, you won't get a call from a client unless something is wrong—unfortunately. "The bill is too high." "The tech took too long." "This is wrong." "That is wrong." It would certainly be great to hear that "the taxes look great" or "the closing went well." And within the office, also, more often than not, complaints will be heard much more frequently than compliments. So, establishing what everyone thinks is really working at a company may take a bit of prodding. But what is working? If any of the staff have longevity with a firm, they must like something. What is it?

Is it the flexible work hours? Is it the work being done? Is it the benefits? The opportunities for growth? The ability to think for oneself and have a decision-making role?

And what do the clients feel is working? The employees working face to face or on the frontline of client support must know the answer and they need to be asked. Do the clients like the service? The products? The workforce? Does the service performed afford them great value? Does it allow them to be more profitable? Do the clients ever list the benefits of the products or the service they receive? Do they make positive comments, such as "great job" or "thanks so much"?

Before looking at everything that is wrong and trying to find some fixes, find out what the company is doing right and do more of the same. The trick is to get some positive thinking going. If the company has been around for a while with clients and employees who have stayed the course, something must be right!

Finding What's Wrong

There's a lot of intuition that can be harnessed from the back office, and when responsible people are empowered, problems can be spotted at the get-go. So, starting with the back-office staff, we need to find out what the employees think is wrong. There is a profit problem; it may also be a sales problem; a cash flow problem; a marketing problem and an everything else problem. A lot is being worked on and change is on the way, but are there back-office rumors about things that are not working?

Is the service not up to par? Is there "dead wood" on the payroll? Are the employees producing value for the customers? Are there people who don't return their phone calls, who come in late and, generally don't care about their job? Why is the company constantly spending more than it is making? Are all the costs being checked? Are sales shrinking? Is the phone not ringing? Are the prices too high? Are the prices too low? Is information at everyone's fingertips? Is the work being done promptly, accurately, without overt babysitting? Is the competition looking better and better to the clients? What needs to be fixed?

Asking the employees who are face to face with clients may produce a different focus. Are they working too many hours? Do they have the proper tools of the trade? Is there a better solution that we can offer the clients? Is the back office supportive? Is there bickering going on? Are our competitors more modern? Is the client base too demanding? Do they think anything is wrong? Or does everything seem right?

Watching the store needs to be on everyone's daily schedule, and no one person can be relied on to keep an eye on everything. From cost control to repeat business, every employee needs to be both a watchdog and a salesperson, saving pennies and helping to bring in the cash.

And, a positive, procompany attitude quickly spreads. There is no room in a small to mid-sized business for constant naysayers, job-haters, and complainers. If going to work is all about what an employee can get instead of what he or she can give, that employee should be in another job.

So, looking around and keeping one's eyes and ears open can go a long way toward change and profit-making behavior. The trick is to engage every employee so that problems or potential problems are identified, not ignored or, worse yet, promoted.

Making It Right

It would be absurd and abnormal to cash a paycheck and throw a few dollars directly into a garbage pail. Yet, many people do just that in their office. Part of the mantra for company success is to protect the company that employs you, being as careful with the company's assets as you would be with your own.

Helping to watch every penny spent, to look for bargains, and to help a company shave expenses should be as routine as watching one's own wallet. Being lean and mean is not just for the boss, but for every single caring employee.

The bottom line is that owning one's job and being the best one can be goes a long way toward fixing most profit problems that are found in the workplace.

Helping the business to keep clients happy, streamline operations, automate processes, and stay up-to-date are all parts of a formula for success that only employees can perform. And, adding ongoing marketing, networking, and sales behavior to the mix, doing an excellent job is more and more about simply caring about your company and caring about your job.

The trick here is pure and simple—be on the income side of the equation, not the expense side. Don't foster apathy; help to find problems and fix problems, always keeping sales and profit in the forefront of the equation.

Joining the Club

If the image of everyone at the office sitting in a circle, holding hands and singing "We Are the World" doesn't seem realistic, here is another example. How about employees personally using the services that are sold, thus swearing by the products that are used? What is needed is complete buy-in and dedication of the staff to the company so that insiders and outsiders both can sense and respect the pride and work ethic behind the door of the business. Now that is a sales team!

Loving one's job, competing together, joining forces with every peer and having success is a powerful energizer. "People power" can't be topped in a service field and mantras aimed at creating a positive, happy, hard-working staff can become welcoming allures.

Weekend athletes can bond on the golf course; football fans can scream in unison at the games; parents of the soccer team can car pool and help to coach. This same team spirit, brought into the workforce, can be a powerful business tool. The trick is to promote and foster a sales team attitude where the success of the business is a direct reflection of the hard-working staff.

In Summary

Sometimes, you have to live through a problem to learn a lesson. For instance, any company suffering with cash flow problems will know the scary fear of not meeting payroll. Turning the office mindset into a sales-thinking office instead of an expense-thinking office can be a big accomplishment and a big step toward turning a better profit. You are not automatically entitled to be a profit-making company. Rather, it takes hard work and the hard work of everyone in the company.

Enlisting the office troops can include:

- Engaging all employees in proactive message spreading both inside and outside the office
- Breaking the mold of rigid job descriptions so all employees can help the company profit
- Promoting excellence in the workforce

Creating a positive company mantra can include:

- Spreading the good news about the company
- Engaging employees in identifying things that are going wrong
- Being on the income side of the business working for sales and profits
- Fostering a sales team attitude that will benefit all

Conclusion

Even though bookshelves are filled with "practice management" guides, the advice within these guides rarely deals with the deep-seated issues surrounding cash and profit. Yet, lack of cash and lack of profit will cause a company to fail no matter what line of business it is in. The dark side of business ownership doesn't get a lot of press: how to stay in business for the long haul; how to survive personal and economic trauma in business; how not to lose everything!

Starting at the end and working backwards, we are looking for a respectable bottom line—to be in the black, not the red. Even though there may be great optimism for future sales and future profits, we are looking right now to revamp, restore, reengineer, and resolve the business issues that result in profit problems.

So, here is a profile of the business being addressed in this book:

- A privately-held firm
- Service-based
- Small to mid-sized
- Needing net profit guidance

A business can be very busy, have a lot of clients, have a good product, deliver a great service, and still have profit problems. Making change now can mean the difference between failing or surviving profitless, and regrouping for net gain and sustainability.

Conclusion

The model of a business seeking net profit advice can run the gamut:

- A successful, profitable business may want to remain profitable, follow trends, avoid pitfalls, understand the market, and seek new profit-making ideas.
- A brand new business, just setting up shop, may want to plan for profitability, set standards for success, stay out of the red, learn from the mistakes of others, and make money.
- A seasoned, long-established business may be suffering the effects of the economy and want to overcome the perils that longevity without innovation has caused. Business may be declining, profits may be shrinking, and the prospects for the long term are not attractive. The expenses are too high for the income being generated, cash flow is suffering, and the current and future business valuations won't be providing for a retirement nest egg. This business needs help.
- A business without longevity may want to create an operable plan for the future, where none currently exists. Right now the business teeters between profits and losses and is banking on tomorrow's business influx to gain success. There's not a lot of focus on the bottom line here. Rather the business switches gears a lot—changing product offerings, trying to come up with new ideas. Staying in business is a day-by-day event.
- A business that is ready to dissolve at any moment may want to try for a turnaround. There may be clients, employees, services, and a market presence, but lack of cash and lack of profits has been hard to overcome.

Different businesses will perform different functions and some solutions are better for one service type business than another.

There are, however, six different steps that can affect change to tighten up and invigorate a service business's bottom line:

- **Step 1: Changing the Rules of Operation.** New sales offerings, expense cutting, and cost-effective restructuring of administration goes into changing the rules of operation. The whole business model gets an overhaul here in order to increase income and at the same time reduce spending. While all new sales methods and offerings are valued, the most strategic change that can be made in the sales arena is switching from a one-time-only sales model to a relationship sales model. Utilizing retainer plans, maintenance contracts, and any other form of prepaid recurring sale that fits your business model will help reduce cash flow problems and enhance the bottom line with an ongoing sales and profit stream.

    Likewise, in the expense and administrative areas, there is one change that is drastically more beneficial than all others—computerization. Not only can manual efforts and expenses be reduced with automation, but, through Job Costing, Time and Billing, and Customer Relationship Management software, profitability, labor utilization, and sales projections can be readily available where before they were not.

- **Step 2: Staying Visible and Connected.** Changing the face that the public sees when they look at your business and connecting you to the outside world is the purpose of evaluating certifications and associations. Even if you have been around for decades, it's important that you stand up to new competition and that your reputation is worn on your sleeve. Increasing marketing-geared credentials and growing new strategic Internet alliances will keep your profile strong and keep your competition in line. And, once you are past the initial sales hook, your experience, competence, and longevity will take over and seal the sales deal. For a seasoned company with questionable profits, it's more important than ever to keep the business resume in top-notch shape and to connect strategically to the outside world.

- **Step 3: Maximizing Cash Flow.** The all-time biggest problem in small to mid-sized business, cash flow, certainly needs attention. Taking the reins and adopting the hardest stance possible can really help create a cash flow turnaround, but it's a tough act. The first task is to create a relationship sales model with ongoing sales of retainer plans and maintenance contracts. If this sales solution doesn't fit your business model, find a similar solution that does. Knowing where your money is coming from and when it will arrive will eliminate sleepless nights and go a long way to resolve your cash flow problems. The next task is to have a solid budget and to tweak it when needed. You need to know what your expenses are, period. There can be no excuse here and, seeing is believing, as far as a budget is concerned. The next task is to know your profit and loss up to the minute. A computer system will help and you will soon live by these numbers but you must gain control and stay in control.
- **Step 4: Streamlining Management Costs.** There is no place in a streamlined business model for an expensive, administrative-heavy back office. With automation, a team of lean and mean managers can concentrate, not on expense-driving tasks, but on expense-saving, income-producing efforts. Primary in benefit is the maintenance of up-to-date, synchronized, shareable information. With accurate data at everyone's fingertips, a sales-oriented office can be more profitable. And, with easy accessibility to client systems, management tasks that the back office performs can become billable client events. Project management, scheduling, and quality control can be an income-producing side effect of a top-notch information management system.
- **Step 5: Raising the Marketing Bar.** Next to cash flow, marketing is paramount to a small to mid-sized business'

success. Often ignored, concentrating on elevating marketing efforts can be immediately rewarding. Using the power of the Internet, new marketing avenues can be explored inexpensively and routinely. And, a fresh face on old, stale marketing pieces and marketing avenues will help keep the "new kids" in their place and remind everyone that you are still around. No matter what marketing methods are used, the most important tool in the marketing equation is the Customer Relationship Management system where all your marketing efforts can be measured directly against new sales and new leads. A return on investment analysis will be at your fingertips with this automation and the measuring of results will allow you to capitalize on marketing successes and immediately eliminate marketing failures.

- **Step 6: Making Everyone a Salesperson**. Stated simply, everyone must help. A sales-minded office will watch the store, cut expenses, give excellent service, and look for sales opportunities. No longer is a job about going to the office and biding your time. Helping with marketing, networking on the web, spreading the word, and promoting good will are all opportunities to help a business be successful. And rigid job descriptions are meant to be broken—today's small to mid-sized business needs all the sales help it can get.

If there is a service business needing to be salvaged, there's a lot that can be changed. Where do you go for help? What do you do first? Can these changes really make the business more profitable? Yes, they can. But, there is no half way. You can't wish the problems away so you need to solve them. Like learning to pay your household bills or live on your allowance or support a family of five, there is income and there is expense. You can't ignore reality.

Starting with sales, getting relationship sales in place is a huge start with cash flow. Down the road, profits will benefit. So, use the word processor, draw up some contracts, and get one retainer plan in place. Then one maintenance contract. Do your research. Find a model that fits your service and do it. Get started with one sale and the rest will follow.

Put someone on cost-cutting ASAP. Cut the phone bills; cut the insurance bills; change your Internet hosting; change your email hosting; cut your payroll service; use an outside backup service and check all the other easy bills that may be reduced. Make a list of all expenses and get on the phone.

Hire a few part-time, flexible experts—someone in accounting; someone to do information technology; someone to manage the office. Does that mean existing staff have to go? You alone can answer that question, but a few high-level tasks need to be done and a few high-level people are needed to do them.

Computerizing is next. Get a better computer system. Yes, do the accounting, but, more importantly, do Job Costing, Time and Billing and, by all means, do Customer Relationship Management—track sales.

A three-month timeline can handle these items—some new sales contracts, the easiest cost cutting, bringing in some high-level staff, and getting more automated.

That leaves everything else! Schedule it all in three-month increments. Make a one-year plan and go through every profit-enhancing step. Then reschedule yearly, quarterly, and monthly reviews, where appropriate.

Hopefully, everyone in the office can passionately embrace this effort and assist with the turnaround. It's worth it!

Appendix A: The How-To Guide to Creating Profit

So theoretically, you buy into the six steps that will have a positive effect on the company's bottom line. And inside these six steps, you see many, many areas where change will help sales, cash flow and, ultimately, profit. But how do you actually accomplish the changes? When should the changes happen? How do you pick and choose what to do and when? There is a lot to do here and we need to find a way to get it done.

There are three processes that need to take place in order to accomplish your goal:

1. Deciding what changes should be made
2. Scheduling the changes
3. Reevaluating each area over and over again in the future

First of all, you need to establish what is happening right now. You need to decide what changes are best, look at alternatives, and make some decisions. Appendix A contains the types of questions that an analyst would ask to help you to decide what changes you need in your business model.

Second, using the Checklist and sample Worksheets contained in Appendix B, you need to prioritize the changes. It would be nice to revamp everything at once but that isn't going to happen. So, setting up four buckets with three months worth of deliverables in each is realistic and effective. Deciding what will be done in each bucket of time is an internal process but there is enough ammunition here to help you realize where the most important changes lie, and when to implement them.

Lastly, as soon as changes begin to be made, you need to immediately establish a schedule for monitoring, measuring, and reevaluating. There must be monthly, quarterly, and yearly ongoing checks of every process.

The marketplace is too volatile for your company to be left unguarded. If there is any lesson to be learned about the problems that are at hand, it should be that this is no time for complacency. The store needs to be watched very carefully if profits are going to be realized.

Deciding What Changes Should Be Made

Going through the six steps outlined in this book, we want to ask some questions, look for some answers, and make decisions about change. Here is an outline that will help you to choose what needs to be analyzed.

Working hand in hand with the Checklist and sample Worksheets in Appendix B, you can be on your way to identifying and instituting real profit-geared change.

Step 1: Changing the Rules of Operation

Increasing Sales
  Questions:
  - What products and services are you currently selling?
  - What products and services did you sell last year, five years ago, ten years ago?
  - Has your sales volume changed? Has it increased? Has it decreased?
  - Are you selling to more customers? Fewer customers?
  - Do the sales come in on their own or do you engage a sales staff?
  - Do your service providers also sell to your clients?
  - Do they upsell?
  - Are you cross-selling goods and services that complement your main offering?

- Are these goods and services that you provide? That other companies provide?
- Are there other goods and services that your competitors add to their mix that you would consider offering?
- Are you a one-time-sale operation or do you sell relationships?
- Do you establish prepaid retainer plans of any kind?
- Do you offer any type of maintenance contracts?
- Do you offer any type of service plans?
- Can you bundle all of the services that you offer into a series of separate plans to sell to your entire client base?
- Can you eliminate all traces of one-time-only sales?
- Do you sell to the general public or do you sell to vertical markets?
- Are your sales offerings things that anyone, anywhere could buy?
- Are your sales geographically targeted?
- What vertical markets are represented in your book of business and can these vertical markets become a larger marketing base?
- If you are not selling to the general public, can you break apart your vertical market offering and attract the general public?
- What exactly is your target market?
- How can this be tweaked to cover a wider area? Or can it be tweaked to represent a smaller, more vertical market area?
- If you sell to large clients, can you target small clients?
- If you sell to small clients, can you target large clients?
- If you sell to a consumer market, can you target a business market?
- If you sell to a business market, can you target a consumer market?
- If you sell to a residential base, can you sell to a commercial base?
- If you sell to a commercial base, can you sell to a residential base?

- What changes are needed for your offerings if you sell to a different market? Does your price go up or down? Does your deliverable get larger or smaller?
- Do you have any low- or no-profit "get in the door" promotions to attract new customers?
- Can you look at your competition and discover other loss leaders to use to attract customers?
- Is there a major new division that you have thought of opening where your brand can attract your client base to a totally new marketing arena?
- Can this brand extension be used to generate clients to your existing business?
- Do you have any successes of the past that have grown stale?
- Are any of your products or services that were once successfully sold now obsolete?
- Can you see how your competitors have replaced their stale sales offerings?
- Can you envision a new sales model for your company incorporating several of these new offerings?

Ideas:
- What changes to your sales offerings should be explored?
- Should you leave your sales model alone?
- Should you decrease your sales offerings?
- Should you increase your sales offerings?

Decreasing Expenses
  Questions:
- Who are all of vendors that you paid money to last year?
- What were the expense categories of each of these payments?
- Can you review this same information for the last several years?
- Can you compare this year's expenses to last year's expenses and find any discrepancies or improper increases?

- In the overhead arena, when was the last time that you price-checked each of these expenses?
- Do you still need every one of these expenses or can some things be eliminated?
- Have some of your standard payables become obsolete?
- Can you renegotiate your rent, if you have a lease?
- If you are the owner, can your real estate taxes be appealed?
- Are all your outsourced services appropriately priced?
- Have you checked for new packaged services with the vendors that you use?
- Have you checked for similar promotions with the competition?
- Is it time to clean up some usage areas such as email mailbox or backup sizes?
- Do you have any obsolete service contracts?
- When you buy new equipment do you add inexpensive long-term service contracts?
- Do you have any contracts on equipment, such as hardware, where replacement is less expensive than repair?
- Are you using older hardware and software that causes some outsourced systems to be more costly?
- Will upgrading your hardware and software allow you to use newer, more inexpensive outsourced services?
- Do you have a postage meter even though you no longer use postage?
- Have you explored replacing insurance policies?
- Are your insurance policies covering the correct people or items?
- Have you reevaluated your hardware insurance coverage to represent lower replacement values?
- Has your workmen's compensation policy been reviewed?
- Do you still need all of the insurance policies that you have in place?
- Are there lower-cost alternatives for bundling some of your insurance plans?

- For costs of goods that may be included in sales to clients, have you checked that the product is not offered for free in another solution?
- Have you checked that your costed items still hold value for your customers?
- Have you checked if your distributor is cost effective in pricing?
- Is a manufacturer selling directly now, possibly at a lower cost?
- Does the manufacturer sell under different labels?
- Should you price-check with different manufacturers?
- Should you price-check with different distributors?
- If you buy all of your products from one manufacturer, will there be price incentives?
- If you buy all of your products from one distributor, will there be price incentives?
- Can your customer buy directly? Have you done appropriate price comparisons?
- Can you find an appropriate enticement so that your customers buy from you and do not buy directly?
- Can you make your vendor your partner with sales incentives, commission incentives, co-op marketing, and lead referrals?
- Can you create a virtual partnership where products are sold to customers but drop-shipped and serviced by the vendor?
- Are the employees who perform your services properly paid?
- Are the employees who perform your services properly trained? Properly certified?
- Is the price that your client pays for a service covering the cost of the employees who perform the service? Does it cover the overhead required?
- Is your back-office service up to date?
- Does your senior staff have proper technical capabilities?
- Does your junior staff have proper managerial capabilities?

- Have you established training, where needed, to elevate the technical level of some employees and the managerial level of other employees?
- Have you done a market analysis of the salaries and benefits of your service providers lately?
- Have you done a market analysis of the salaries and benefits of your back office employees lately?
- Are your expenses rising while your sales are not?
- Are your employees being paid more and performing less?
- Do you have the right combination of service providers, senior staff, junior staff, technical staff, and nontechnical staff?

Ideas:
- What expense changes should be explored?
- Should you leave your expenses alone?
- Should you reduce your expenses?
- Should you increase your expenses?

Streamlining Administration
Questions:
- What functions in your company are performed manually?
- What parts of your company are computerized?
- What parts of your computer system are integrated with each other?
- Should your manual operations remain manual or is there a reason to add more computer functions?
- Have you had an analysis of your hardware done recently?
- Are you spending too much money to maintain older equipment?
- Could there be a cost-effective reason to upgrade old hardware?
- Have you had an analysis of your software done lately?
- Are you spending too much money to maintain older software?

- What new software tools or hardware tools would make your back-office staff more productive?
- Have you done a return-on-investment analysis of newer computer software?
- Do you even know what new software exists for your industry?
- Does your service-providing staff have the proper tools of the trade?
- Are you administration heavy? Could computerizing reduce staff?
- Is your accounting system automated?
- Do you handle quotations, budgets, sales orders, purchase orders, checks, bank reconciliations, receivables, payables, general ledger, and financial statements?
- Do you have an automated budget versus actual analysis?
- Do you have access to a computerized profit and loss analysis?
- Do you have a generic, nonproprietary computer software solution from a reputable vendor?
- Do you have a Job Costing system where income and expense is measured on a job-by-job basis?
- Do you have a Time and Billing system where each of your employees breaks their labor down client by client and job by job?
- Are you doing a labor utilization analysis comparing labor performed by each employee to work hours?
- Do you have a Customer Relationship Management system where sales information for new and existing clients is managed?
- Does your Customer Relationship Management system integrate with your sales?
- Are you tracking salesperson information?
- What processes are you outsourcing?
- Have you checked the prices of outsourced functions lately?
- Are you outsourcing payroll, website hosting, email hosting, system backups, and hardware maintenance?

- Are your employees spending too much time on administrative, non-client-related functions?
- Can you outsource more functions such as software development, report writing, website development, electronic buying and selling (Ecommerce and EDI)?
- Are your employees properly trained to optimize software use?
- Are your employees' systems standardized for ease of use and maintenance?
- Are your employees using free or low cost outsourced e-learning for their training needs?
- Are your main marketing functions being outsourced, especially mass emailing, newsletter preparation, direct mailers, telemarketing, ad creation, and press releases?
- Have you price checked and value checked all of your outsourced processes?
- Have you looked at your office expenses to see if there are any other outsourcing opportunities?
- Can you create a more virtual office?
- Can you use a Virtual Assistant, telecommuting and handling your administration needs?
- Do you need to perform all of the administrative tasks that you have been performing or can you streamline more?
- Can your in-house staff become more client focused and less administratively focused?
- Have you checked what each employee is doing and make sure it still has value?
- How many administrators do you have and what are their functions?
- Do you have any office manuals?
- Are they all in one place?
- Do you have a manual for problem solving and client relations?
- Does your manual cover employee rules, regulations, benefits, agreements, office expectations, and client deliverables?

- Does your manual cover all client matters such as contracts, pricing, collections, service matters, and customer service?
- Does your manual cover vendor information, marketing management, and accounting?
- Does your manual standardize office procedures?
- Do you have a need for high level administrative help?
- Do you need a Managing Director, an Office Manager, an Accountant, a CFO, a CIO, or a Sales Director?
- Have you explored a senior part-time, flexible workforce?
- Would there be a greater return on investment if you hired part-time senior staff?
- Will streamlining your office create a more sales oriented, client service organization?

Ideas:
- What streamlining changes should be explored?
- Should administration be left alone?
- Should the administration be reduced?
- Should the administration be enhanced?

Step 2: Staying Visible and Connected

Increasing Credentials
Questions:
- What credentials does your business have?
- Have you had these same credentials for years?
- Did you have different credentials in the past?
- How do you compare to your competitors as far as credentials are concerned?
- How does a customer know about your credentials?
- What mandatory professional licenses must you have?
- What mandatory vendor certifications must you have?
- Are there other accreditations, certifications, licenses, or stamps of approval that could market your company's credibility?
- Have you researched these areas lately?

- Which of these are cost-effective to obtain?
- Are some of these credentials too expensive to maintain?
- Have you done a return-on-investment analysis with regard to these credentials?
- Are there additional vendor-related certifications that will increase your lead referrals?
- Are there additional vendor-related certifications that will offer you discounted services?
- What types of industry and professional certifications are most suited to marketing your wares?
- Are there vertical market accreditations that you can obtain?
- Are there any memberships in elite organizations that will gain your company recognition?
- Has your company received any awards?
- Have your competitors received awards?
- What awards might you try to attain?
- Are there lists that magazines and newspapers construct that would market your strengths?
- Should public relations specialists assist you in seeking awards?
- Have you checked associations, organizations, and national magazines and publications for awards you may deserve?
- Do your employees have credentials that you should market?
- Are your employees vendor certified? Industry certified?
- Do your employees have advanced degrees?
- Have your employees been recognized for excellence in the past?
- Should you separate out your employees for recognition? Inside the office? Outside the office?
- Should you create collective company-wide stats about employees such as years of experience or certification strengths?
- Should you recognize your employee's personal athletic or charitable accomplishments?

- Is there a great benefit to include your employees in your marketing efforts?
- Do you have a certification path for your employees?
- Do you have a recognition path for your employees?
- Is building your company's resume important to you?
- Was your company's resume important in the past and has the focus slipped?

Ideas:
- What company credentials should be explored?
- Should your company credentials be left alone?
- Should your company credentials be increased?
- Should your company credentials be decreased?

Growing Affiliations
Questions:
- What associations does your company belong to?
- What official affiliations does your company have?
- Has this changed over time?
- What associations and affiliations did you have last year? Five years ago? Ten years ago?
- Are you a dues-paying member of any associations?
- Are you actively involved in these associations?
- Is there value in continuing membership?
- What other associations exist in the marketplace?
- What kind of strategic alliances are modern companies establishing?
- Are you using the Internet to explore available alliances?
- Are you using the Internet to create alliances?
- Are you known as an expert in your field?
- Have you explored establishing your company as an expert in the media, online, on television, on radio?
- Have you written a news column in the past for a newspaper or other publication?
- What online publications are available?
- Can you write online news columns?
- Have you explored online ad sharing?

- Should you be an advertisement on other websites?
- Should you allow other vendors to have ads on your website?
- Are you creating online marketing referrals?
- What other online marketing referrals are available?
- Are you generating traffic to your website?
- Should you explore search engine optimization techniques?
- Are you using Google Analytics or other website tools to track the sources of your web traffic?
- Are you making marketing adjustments based on the results of this website tracking?
- Are your employees and your company listed on available social and business online network sites?
- Are you quickly mastering new Internet alliance-building tools?
- Have you cleaned up shop and removed any old, stale, ineffective associations or alliances?

Ideas:
- What associations and affiliations should your company explore?
- Should the associations and affiliations that you have be left alone?
- Should they be increased?
- Should they be decreased?

Step 3: Maximizing Cash Flow

Keeping the Cash Flowing
Questions:
- Do you have cash flow problems?
- Have you had these problems for a year? For years? Forever?
- Do you know what your cash flow needs are? Every week? Every month? Every year?

- Do you have a steady stream of cash coming into your business?
- Is your cash intake sporadic and nonpredictable?
- Do you work on net 30 day terms? Do the terms stretch to 60 days? 90 days? Longer?
- Does your profit disappear because your cost of collections, interest, and expense eat up the bottom line?
- Do you have specific low cash flow months?
- Do you have specific high cash flow months?
- Do your competitors use the same terms as you use with your clients?
- What kind of prepaid retainer plans do you have or can you establish?
- Can you make a plan to turn all client labor into prepaid retainer plan labor?
- Can you offer clients incentives to work in a retainer plan model?
- What competitive services can be offered in a retainer plan model?
- Do you hire and fire based on the number of contracted clients that you have?
- What other prepaid bundles, such as maintenance contracts can you establish?
- Do you tightly manage employee work schedules?
- Do you coordinate work schedules with collections?
- Do you coordinate work schedules with impending sales?
- Do you coordinate work schedules with impending contract renewals and retainer plan payments?
- Can you manage new client efforts, large job efforts, and normal weekly work keeping cash flow in mind?
- What income do you have that is not from a sale to a client?
- Do you manage vendor and cross-selling commission income?
- Do you manage referral-based income?
- Do you have procedures in place to order goods and services around work schedules?

- Do you have procedures in place to order goods and services around cash flow and credit availability?
- Do you manage Accounts Payable with friendly credit terms?
- Can you list all of your vendors and the payment term arrangements that you have with them?
- Do you have senior staff seek out more favorable terms with vendors?
- Do you change vendors if better payment terms are available elsewhere?
- Do you manage your payments due around credit card statement dates, also aiming for no interest fees?
- Do you stretch cash flow by reselling low-profit-margin goods?
- Is your purchasing agent cognizant of ordering goods "just in time" for their use?
- Is your purchasing agent savvy with your payment processes?
- Are returns handled properly and promptly?
- Do you receive all of the refunds that you deserve?
- Do you receive all of the co-op funding that you deserve?
- Can cash flow be managed differently?

Ideas:
- What cash flow management changes can you explore?
- Should collections, payments, and cash flow be left alone?
- Should changes be put in place?

Knowing Your Budget
Questions:
- Do you have a budget?
- Have you had a budget in the past?
- Can you compare this year's budget with previous years' budgets?
- Do you have a senior bookkeeper or controller investigating and managing your budget?
- Do you properly budget for sales?

- Do you have a reliable sales budgeting formula?
- Are you projecting sales to new clients based on last year's sales?
- Do you consider new marketing avenues and new sales offerings in your sales budget?
- Are you budgeting for sales to new clients?
- Are you budgeting for sales to existing clients?
- Are you including all non-client-related income in your sales budget such as commissions and referral fees?
- Are you evaluating all existing retainer plan, maintenance contract, and other recurring client billing in your sales budget?
- Are you projecting growth in these relationship sales categories? Are you trying to eliminate all one-time billing models?
- Have you reviewed all of last year's expenses?
- Have you compared these expenses to previous years' expenses?
- Were you able to review previous year's budget to actual comparisons?
- Can you categorize your expenses as fixed, sales-dependent, and discretionary?
- For fixed expenses, have you included all administrative payments made last year and updated the costs based on this year's projections?
- Have you finished an expense review and removed any unnecessary expenses?
- For sales-dependent costs, have you included all presales efforts, such as entertainment, auto, and gas expense?
- For sales-dependent costs, have you included potential credit card expense should a customer pay their bill on a charge card?
- For sales-dependent costs, have you included all costs of labor, in-house and outsourced?
- For discretionary expenses, have you included all owner benefits that will not be covered if profit does not exist?

- For discretionary expenses, have you included all potential entertainment, gifts, donations, and other discretionary costs?
- For discretionary expenses have you included possible bonuses?
- Have you reconciled your planned income to your planned expenses and created a profit balance? A loss balance?
- Do you have the ability to prepare actual versus budget calculations on an ongoing basis?
- Do you have the ability to tweak all budget items through the year when discrepancies or changes are discovered?

Ideas:
- What budget changes should be explored?
- Do the budgeted sales need to be increased?
- Do the budgeted sales need to be decreased?
- Do the budgeted expenses need to be increased?
- Do the budgeted expenses need to be decreased?
- Is profit and loss capture acceptable?
- Is budget versus actual capture acceptable?

Working to the Bottom Line
Questions:
- Do you understand Job Costing?
- Do you have a Job Costing system?
- Does it integrate to all other office systems?
- Do you have a history of job cost analysis on previous sales?
- Do you create budgeted job costs?
- Do you measure budgeted versus actual job costs?
- Do you create new prices for customers without calculating job cost budgets?
- Do you know if your jobs are profitable or not?
- Do you know which sales produce profits and which sales produce losses?

- Do you know which customers produce profitable sales and which customers don't?
- Do you understand Time and Billing analysis?
- Do you maintain a Time and Billing system?
- Does it integrate to all other office systems?
- Do you post all client-related labor for all employees to a Time and Billing system?
- Is the client-related employee labor attributed to the proper clients?
- Can you measure employee down time and overhead time? Do you calculate net profit on each job after posting all applicable costs and labor?
- Do you know the up-to-the-minute profit and loss at your company? On a job-by-job basis? On a client-by-client basis?
- Do you know the profit and loss on a month-to-month basis? Year to year?
- Do you know the labor utilization at your company?
- Are employees billing clients 50% of their time? 80% of their time? 20% of their time?
- Can you compare labor utilization rates by the week, by the month, by the year, employee to employee, client to client, job to job?
- Are employees having low utilization rates because there is not enough work to do? Because the jobs are not priced properly? Because they are not productive?
- Do you create deliverable objectives for your employees with job costing and labor utilization figures in hand?
- Are you measuring the information that results in profit creation?

Ideas:
- What processes should be explored in order for you to work more efficiently toward the bottom line?
- Are changes needed?

- Should processes be changed?
- Should processes be left alone?
- Do you have accurate profit and loss analysis, job cost analysis and labor utilization analysis in place?

Step 4: Streamlining Management Costs

Changing the Back-Office Focus
Questions:
- Has the back office operated as an expense to the company?
- Can the back office be changed to a sales-driving, customer service support, and customer service center?
- What are the processes that are in place for data entry and information management?
- Is system integration tightly in place eliminating redundant data entry?
- Is the staff trained so that proper procedures take place to eliminate redundancy?
- How timely is data entry and data management?
- Can you establish extremely timely management of administrative and financial data?
- Can this administrative and financial data be synchronized so that a full, timely company-wide picture is always available?
- Can you establish extremely timely management of all employee, client, and vendor data?
- Can you establish extremely timely management of all Job Cost and Time and Billing data entry?
- Can you revisit budget changes in a very timely fashion?
- Can you manage up-to-the-minute Customer Relationship Management information so that sales projections are accurate?
- Can you oversee up-to-date, synchronized data management leading to accurate Profit and Loss, Sales, Cash Flow, Job Profitability, and Labor Utilization reporting?

- What business management reporting is needed and is it readily available?
- On a less urgent basis, can you manage updating accurate tech support information, training requirements, vendor information, office procedures, and sales information?
- Can you manage timely marketing updates for employees and clients?
- Can the company website be updated more frequently and with time-sensitive information?
- Can you produce timely reporting on client spending and profits month by month and year by year?
- Can you produce alerts when clients have not been using your services?
- Can you produce timely, accurate reporting on open purchase orders, client contract renewals, cash flow projections, and the source of new customer leads?
- What outsourced processes need management by the back office?
- Do you use outsourced software updating, security monitoring, offsite backups, hardware management, email hosting, website hosting, and Internet service?
- Do you make sure that there is no additional outsourced spending without approval?
- Do you manage that functions are properly performing?
- Do you manage Internet advertising spending carefully?
- Do you manage online recruiting spending carefully?
- Are in-house processes being managed carefully by the back-office staff?
- Are important company contracts and authorizations scanned and stored safely?
- Is there a double storage system of important information so that electronic storage has a hard copy backup?
- Is tight security in effect for company computer systems?
- Are employees cognizant of policies surrounding use of company equipment?
- Is there electronic reporting and management of company system use?

- Is company data properly managed?
- Is the office information system networked and available for employee use at all times?
- Is company-wide procedural, employee, client, and vendor information shareable?
- Is client history, contract, proposal, accounting, and job-related information shareable?
- Is vendor-specific product, history, and technical support information shareable?
- Are the company website and other online company systems used for contact, calendar, and data sharing?
- Is the back office properly supporting the company-wide systems?

Ideas:
- What back office processes should be evaluated?
- Should back office processes be left alone?
- Should back office processes be reduced?
- Should back office processes be enhanced?
- What is the return on investment with the back-office functions?

Managing for Profit
Questions:
- Which employees participate in client-billing work and which employees do not?
- Is there client work that is not represented in invoices to clients?
- When analyzing the cost of doing a job are all labor-related costs actually being included?
- Does the back-office staff perform actual client-related project management tasks?
- Does the proper information management allow administrators to perform job-related scheduling, follow-up, and managerial tasks?
- Is this time being included in the costing of the jobs?

- Are there senior management employees who spend their days working on client-related tasks, fighting fires, and supporting face-to-face technicians?
- Is this senior management time attributed to the costing of the client job?
- Do you bill your clients with fixed prices, such as for weekly services or standard functions?
- For these fixed-price jobs, does it matter how much labor is involved?
- Will the customer pay the same price no matter what time it takes?
- For these types of jobs, when the prices are established, are you budgeting for all labor costs, including all costs of goods?
- Are the back-office managers who work directly on a specific client job having their time allocated and included in the budget of the job?
- Are the senior managers who act as a support reference for face-to-face service providers having their time properly allocated to the cost of a job?
- Do you have budget versus actual comparisons of your fixed-price jobs? Can you see the anticipated costs of labor contained in these jobs and the actual labor that took place?
- Are your prices too low and not covering actual costs?
- Will your clients pay more for these services?
- Do you need to reduce labor components or cost of goods allocated in order to maintain current pricing in light of actual costs?
- For hourly billed jobs, again, are all the back-office employees and the senior behind-the-scene managers having their time properly posted to the job at hand?
- Is it acceptable in your industry to include back-office and behind-the-scene charges on your hourly bills?
- Should you establish a flat-fee management cost that is directly invoiced to the client that would cover these back-office and senior-management costs?

- Would this be cost effective and user-friendly to the client?
- Do you have a one-tier billing system where every service provider costs the same amount to a client?
- Should you create tiered billing rates so that senior managers have a higher value than junior service providers and back-office managers also carry a different rate?
- Are there any other lost profit centers that are not being accounted for in the costing of your jobs?
- Can you purposely develop a more client-billable back-office using an improved information management system?

Ideas:
- What management costs should be explored?
- Should the in-house processes remain the same?
- Should billing practices remain the same?
- Will proper use of Job Costing and Time and Billing systems result in costing, pricing, and billing changes?

Step 5: Raising the Marketing Bar

Networking
Questions:
- What traditional networking avenues have been utilized?
- What networking avenues are employed now versus one year ago? Five years ago? Ten years ago?
- Are face-to-face networking encounters fading?
- Have Internet networking opportunities been explored?
- What are they and are they cost effective and time effective?
- Does the company use online social and business networking sites?
- Are business profiles created for employees as well as the company?
- Are business networking sites utilized for sales, marketing, recruiting and business networking?
- Has a profile been posted on Wikipedia?
- Have business videos been posted on YouTube?

- Is Twitter being used by the business and are you following Twitter updates of other business peers?
- What traditional networking avenues do your competitors utilize?
- What about online networking by your competitors?
- Do you follow any business-oriented blogs?
- Have you researched other small business or similar business blogs?
- Can you set up a company blog?
- Can you use the blog for marketing purposes?
- Can some Internet-savvy, knowledgeable employees manage the blog?
- Have you created news columns in the past?
- Can you contribute to online news outlets?
- Have you explored what online news publications are appropriate?
- Can you use the online news articles for marketing purposes?
- Have you explored the benefits of using online networks, Wikipedia, YouTube, blogs, and online news articles for search engine optimization?
- Have you followed Google Analytics to determine which of these online networking areas send the most traffic to your website?
- When you search your name or your company name using a search engine can you see which of these online networks appears most often in the result?
- What marketing efforts do you need to establish to connect your customers and potential customers to all of your online networks?
- Does your company use web conferencing to connect to clients or potential clients?
- Do you use web conferencing for your own business needs?
- Can you leverage face-to-face time by reducing meetings and conferences, replacing them with web conferencing?

- What are the best web conferences to use?
- Can you establish standard daily, weekly, or monthly web sales conferences?
- Can participants be invited globally or nationally?
- Can web conferencing be used for presentations, meetings, training, and even support services?
- What presentation skills need development in order to capture the participant's interest and hold the interest?
- What online forums are available for your market space?
- Is there a respectable business community that can be accessed through an online forum?
- Is there an Internet-savvy employee who can field questions, offer advice, and gain credibility on an online forum?
- What news outlets, vendors, and private domains offer appropriate forums for your business connections?
- Have you researched webcasts?
- Do you attend webcasts where major announcements occur or wide audiences are reached?
- Can you use webcasts as a marketing or sales event?
- Can you present product or service announcements using webcasts?
- Have you researched podcasts?
- Have you looked at the large libraries of available business podcasts?
- Should your company invest in a series of lectures, training sessions, or other sales or marketing tools using podcasts?
- Are there employees who might be naturals for both webcasts and podcasts?

Ideas:
- What changes to your networking should be explored?
- Should networking efforts remain the same?
- Should networking efforts be reduced?
- Should networking efforts be enhanced?

Covering All Bases
Questions:

- Do you have a marketing plan?
- Have you had a plan for years?
- Can you compare this year's plan with last year's plan? With the plan from five years ago? From ten year's ago?
- Does your business survive on word of mouth and references?
- Do you have a marketing budget?
- Have you revisited your standard business presentations?
- Are your business cards, letterhead, envelopes, and brochures up to date and high quality?
- Is your website updated?
- Are you listed in online Internet registries?
- Are all of your online business profiles updated?
- Do you use syndicated material and vendor material for your website content?
- Are you properly linked with your affiliates' websites?
- Do your marketing tools compare favorably to your competitors?
- Have you looked at new start-ups lately?
- Do they have a more modern look and feel to their marketing efforts?
- Does your company profile and marketing image convey the experience and longevity that your company has to offer?
- Do you have YouTube, LinkedIn, and Facebook presence?
- What kind of traditional advertising have you done?
- Is it still cost effective?
- Are you using vendor co-op funds for print ads and newsletter preparation?
- Are you using online advertising and are you monitoring it?
- Are you using cross-linking between complementary service providers?
- Are you using online tools that allow you to preempt your competitors on search engines?

- Are you using direct mail pieces and mailing newsletters?
- Should you use email-only services, utilizing all-in-one mass email shops?
- Are you using your brand as an advertisement on marketing items and as credits where you do business?
- Have you explored radio and television opportunities?
- Are you outsourcing the most sophisticated pieces of your marketing plan?
- Are you using article placement and press releases effectively?
- Are you promoting your good will and philanthropic efforts?
- Do you teach classes, give speeches, and serve as a professional reference?
- What kinds of referrals does your company receive?
- Can you enhance and formalize your referrals?
- Do vendors provide referrals?
- Are there private service agencies that can be utilized to broker references?
- Should you solicit recommendations and market them to your vendors and your potential clients?
- What direct contact marketing are you still using?
- Do you attend trade shows and conferences?
- Do you make presentations to prospective clients?
- Do you utilize web conferencing as a face-to-face marketing forum?
- Do you provide services and lectures for continuing education venues where a great deal of marketing is utilized?
- Are there smaller venues such as local bookstores or local associations where your lectures will be appreciated?
- Do you still employ in-house or outsourced telemarketers?
- Do your salespeople still cold-call and engage in direct sales efforts?
- Do you have a marketing presence that is appropriate for your business model?

Ideas:
- What changes to your marketing efforts should be explored?
- Should all marketing be left alone?
- Should you decrease some of your marketing efforts?
- Should you increase other marketing efforts?

Strategizing
Questions:
- What marketing strategies have you followed in the past?
- What return-on-investment analysis have you explored?
- Are you satisfied with previous marketing efforts?
- Do you know what has been successful and what has not been successful?
- Do you have a Customer Relationship Management system in place?
- Is it integrated with the sales side of your accounting system?
- Does it provide reporting tools on sales projections, salesperson activity, and client activity?
- Can you equate every sale with the relevant marketing tool used?
- Is every client and every lead that you have ever had entered into your system?
- Do you have the source of every client and every lead? Do you know how you originally connected with each of these people?
- Do you have a process in place to track every new sales contact according to their source?
- Do you have a process in place to track every new sale according to the marketing plan used?
- Are you ensuring that no client or prospective client is entered into your records without the proper tracking information?

- Can you measure your contact with strangers?
- Are you using a mass email company that can provide you with statistics on how many people read your newsletter or email?
- Are you using Google Analytics to track how many people entered your website and how long they spent browsing?
- If you use telemarketers, are you measuring their contacts with prospective clients?
- When you market to your own list of leads are you tracking how many people reacted to your marketing efforts?
- How many of these people began doing business with you?
- If you are not able to directly judge the success rate of a marketing program (such as a television exposure), are you able to notice any measurable increase in your website audience or inbound prospect calls at that time?
- Have you developed the judgment necessary to weigh subtle marketing success or failure?
- Can you statistically compare marketing efforts to sales efforts?
- Can you use these results to change marketing paths?

Ideas:
- What strategies can be explored to judge marketing success?
- Should you leave marketing programs intact?
- Should you make changes based on sales statistics?

Step 6: Making Everyone a Salesperson

Enlisting the Troops
   Questions:
- Is every employee aware of the sales-oriented business model as opposed to the expense-oriented business model?

- Have new sales-oriented training sessions been established?
- Who is in charge of office processes and what monitoring is happening?
- Are the phones properly answered? Are phone calls always returned? Are emails answered promptly?
- Does everyone have a positive attitude?
- Are all office communications professional in nature?
- Are emails utilized as marketing tools with signature lines, reference links, and neat, professional content?
- Is there a professional dress code policy that everyone is following?
- Are all Internet business profiles being maintained?
- Is office behavior always professional in nature without constant texting and cell phone use?
- Are all office systems used according to office policy?
- Is all business information treated as proprietary and secure?
- Is there a balance in the office between job responsibilities and company-enhancing contributions?
- Can some employees step out of their defined roles and participate in marketing activities such as website use and online networking?
- Are people thinking outside of the box and helping to create sales and marketing opportunities?
- When you recruit for new employees, do searches reveal possible sales leads?
- Can market research be squeezed into someone's job so that competing companies, as well as potential sales opportunities, are recognized?
- Are new ideas fostered with the employees?
- Is there a standard of excellence in the office?
- Is there an opportunity for growth within the company?
- Can an employee explore new avenues by writing news articles, obtaining new certifications, and thinking outside the box?

Ideas:
- What changes to office culture should be explored?
- Are employees on-board with a sales-oriented culture?
- Should things be left alone?
- Are there things that need to be changed?

Creating a Mantra
Questions:
- What is the overall attitude in the office?
- Are there employees who have insight about problem-solving and profitability issues?
- Are managers involved in recommending changes that could be client service oriented?
- When was the last time that back-office management was asked for some advice?
- Are there rumors around the office that can shed some light on procedures that are not working?
- Can you find out what is working with the client base?
- Can you find out what is working with the employees?
- Does everyone like the services that you provide?
- Do they like the products that you sell?
- Are clients generally happy?
- Are employees generally happy?
- Is there a competing solution that should be explored?
- Are there certain service providers who do not provide proper care to clients?
- Why is the company spending more than it is receiving?
- Do certain people need constant assistance and babysitting?
- Who is the company watchdog?
- Can there be more watchdogs?
- Can entrepreneurial behavior spread to the employees?
- Can pleasing the client, enhancing sales, and watching the bottom line become the company mantra?
- Can the company be marketed from within?

Ideas:
- What positive thinking should be explored?
- Should more people become involved in promoting the company from within?
- Should things be left alone?
- Should changes be made?

Appendix B: Scheduling the Changes

While answering the questions in Appendix A, working with a spreadsheet to organize and plan your profit-geared changes will help you to schedule and actually attain the goals that you set.

Actually scheduling change requires not only a decision to deeply analyze business processes in order to establish a new model, but a serious prioritizing of which items to tackle first and which items to schedule for the future. Prioritizing, more often than not, will be impacted by the time commitment needed by key employees. So, focusing premium efforts on premium problems is certainly the goal.

Here is a sample Checklist which allows you to mark an item for change analysis. The few sample Worksheets can be used to model your own spreadsheets and organize your own internal schedules. Quarterly deliverable buckets can be established with Quarter 1 containing the most time-sensitive, profit-enhancing changes and Quarter 4 containing the changes that either piggy-back on earlier accomplishments or, if standing alone, can wait the longest amount of time.

Of course, every business is different. While these sample Worksheets plan deliverables in yearly quarters, your business may need less time or more time for each block of work.

When the Checklist is complete, you will have identified what you want to tackle. Next comes the actual nitty-gritty of assigning these items to responsible task masters.

You will need to judge which employees can be utilized and the amount of time each of these people can devote to this work. Using 10 work hours per week for 46 working weeks per year allows 115 hours ($10 \times 46/4$) per quarter for profit-enhancing change. A lot can be accomplished in 115 hours.

You will need to massage your deliverable list based on available "helpers" and available time. The message, however, needs to be clear—this needs to happen!

Checklist

Step 1: Changing the Rules of Operation

Increasing Sales

- ☐ Review products and services that you sell
- ☐ Review your historical sales offerings
- ☐ Sell additional products
- ☐ Sell additional services
- ☐ Add new customers
- ☐ Reduce customers
- ☐ Hire sales staff
- ☐ Train service providers to sell
- ☐ Upsell products and services
- ☐ Cross-sell your own complementary goods
- ☐ Cross-sell your own complementary services
- ☐ Cross-sell goods from other vendors
- ☐ Cross-sell services from other vendors
- ☐ Copy competitors' product offerings
- ☐ Copy competitors' service offerings
- ☐ Establish a relationship sales model
- ☐ Establish prepaid retainer plans
- ☐ Establish maintenance contracts
- ☐ Establish service plans
- ☐ Bundle existing services into new plans
- ☐ Retire your one-time-only sales model

☐ Sell to the masses
☐ Sell to new vertical markets
☐ Establish new global dominance
☐ Establish new geographic dominance
☐ Expand on existing vertical markets
☐ Break vertical sales into generic offerings
☐ Enhance your existing target market
☐ Expand sales to larger clients
☐ Expand sales to smaller clients
☐ Expand to a business to consumer market
☐ Expand to a business to business market
☐ Expand to residential customers
☐ Expand to commercial customers
☐ Increase your prices
☐ Decrease your prices
☐ Increase the size of your offerings
☐ Decrease the size of your offerings
☐ Establish "get in the door" promos
☐ Copy competitors' "get in the door" promos
☐ Use your brand to market a different solution
☐ Reap core business clients from the new solution
☐ Retire stale product or service offerings
☐ Replace stale product or service offerings
☐ Copy competitors' new product offerings
☐ Copy competitors' new service offerings
☐ Develop a new sales model around your changes

Decreasing Expenses
☐ Review all of your vendors
☐ Review all vendor expense categories
☐ Review vendor deliverables
☐ Review vendor rates
☐ Compare previous year vendor spending
☐ Obtain competitive quotes for all expenses
☐ Review vendor relevance
☐ Review all leases
☐ Review real estate tax payments

Appendix B: Scheduling the Changes

- ☐ Review building maintenance fees
- ☐ Review bundled services with current vendors
- ☐ Review bundled services with new vendors
- ☐ Review all existing outsourced costs
- ☐ Review all existing outsourced deliverables
- ☐ Review relevance of all existing outsourced items
- ☐ Review any existing service contracts
- ☐ Add hardware contracts to all new hardware
- ☐ Review all old hardware maintenance expense
- ☐ Review all old software maintenance expense
- ☐ Price check new hardware and software
- ☐ Review postage needs
- ☐ Review all insurance policies
- ☐ Check hardware insurance coverage
- ☐ Review workmen's compensation policy
- ☐ Review relevance of all insurance coverage
- ☐ Verify relevance of product offerings
- ☐ Price check all costs of goods with distributors
- ☐ Price check all costs of goods with manufacturers
- ☐ Price check for alternate labels
- ☐ Negotiate with manufacturers and distributors
- ☐ Determine the benefits of using a single supplier
- ☐ Compare any customer-direct pricing
- ☐ Offer benefits for non-customer-direct sales
- ☐ Make vendors into partners for marketing
- ☐ Make vendors into partners for sales
- ☐ Review vendor co-op programs
- ☐ Review vendor lead referral programs
- ☐ Establish virtual partnerships with vendors
- ☐ Review service provider salaries
- ☐ Review service provider training programs
- ☐ Review service provider certifications
- ☐ Review customer prices versus costs of goods
- ☐ Review customer prices versus labor costs
- ☐ Review customer prices versus overhead costs
- ☐ Review modern back office services
- ☐ Review technical skills of back-office staff

Checklist

- [ ] Review managerial skills of back-office staff
- [ ] Establish back-office technical-training models
- [ ] Establish back-office managerial-training models
- [ ] Analyze service provider salaries
- [ ] Analyze service provider benefits
- [ ] Analyze back-office salaries
- [ ] Analyze back-office benefits
- [ ] Review pricing increases versus cost increases
- [ ] Review service provider deliverables
- [ ] Review back-office deliverables
- [ ] Review staffing of service providers
- [ ] Review staffing of back office

Streamlining Administration

- [ ] Review all manual office processes
- [ ] Review all computerized office processes
- [ ] Review integration of computerized processes
- [ ] Establish wish list for automation
- [ ] Obtain hardware upgrade quotations
- [ ] Review existing hardware maintenance costs
- [ ] Obtain software upgrade quotations
- [ ] Review existing software maintenance costs
- [ ] Review applicable hardware office solutions
- [ ] Review applicable software office solutions
- [ ] Review cost-effectiveness of new office solutions
- [ ] Review state-of-the art technological solutions
- [ ] Perform a ROI technological analysis
- [ ] Review tools in place for service providers
- [ ] Review tools in place for administrators
- [ ] Review administrative staffing
- [ ] Review the complete accounting system
- [ ] Review quotations, budgets, sales orders
- [ ] Review purchase orders, checks, receivables
- [ ] Review bank reconciliations, payables
- [ ] Review general ledger, financial statements
- [ ] Review budget versus actual analyses
- [ ] Review profit and loss analyses

☐ Review relevant financial software solutions
☐ Establish Job Costing requirements
☐ Establish Time and Billing requirements
☐ Establish Labor Utilization requirements
☐ Establish CRM requirements
☐ Establish Salesperson tracking needs
☐ Review additional outsourced options
☐ Review additional outsourcing prices
☐ Review additional outsourcing deliverables
☐ Review outsourced payroll
☐ Review outsourced website hosting
☐ Review outsourced email hosting
☐ Review outsourced computer backups
☐ Review outsourced hardware maintenance
☐ Review Internet access costs
☐ Review administrative deliverables
☐ Review client-related work deliverables
☐ Review outsourced software development
☐ Review outsourced report writing
☐ Review outsourced website development
☐ Review outsourced Ecommerce
☐ Review outsourced EDI
☐ Review software optimization programs
☐ Establish standardized internal software use
☐ Review e-learning offerings
☐ Review outsourced mass emailing
☐ Review outsourced newsletter preparation
☐ Review outsourced direct mailing
☐ Review outsourced telemarketing
☐ Review outsourced ad creation
☐ Review outsourced press releases
☐ Review employee telecommuting options
☐ Review Virtual Assistant offerings
☐ Streamline administrative tasks
☐ Eliminate non-service-oriented tasks
☐ Manage and update office manuals
☐ Establish problem-solving protocol

- ☐ Establish client relations protocol
- ☐ Establish office protocol
- ☐ Establish employee protocol
- ☐ Establish vendor relations protocol
- ☐ Document all office material
- ☐ Document all client relations material
- ☐ Document all employee material
- ☐ Document all vendor relations material
- ☐ Document marketing management
- ☐ Document accounting processes
- ☐ Establish standardized procedures
- ☐ Measure high level back-office staffing needs
- ☐ Establish a high level chain of command
- ☐ Explore a high level part-time workforce
- ☐ Explore a flexible workforce
- ☐ Create a sales oriented, client service company

Step 2: Staying Visible and Connected

Increasing Credentials

- ☐ Review current company credentials
- ☐ Review historical company credentials
- ☐ Compare credentials to those of competitors
- ☐ Review marketing of credentials
- ☐ Review required professional licenses
- ☐ Review mandatory vendor certifications
- ☐ Research credibility-based accreditations
- ☐ Review cost-effectiveness of all accreditations
- ☐ Review competitive values of all accreditations
- ☐ Perform an ROI credential analysis
- ☐ Review optional vendor certifications
- ☐ Review vendor credentials for lead generation
- ☐ Review vendor credentials for discounts
- ☐ Review available industry certifications
- ☐ Review available professional certifications
- ☐ Review vertical market accreditations
- ☐ Review memberships in elite organizations

- ☐ Review all previously earned awards
- ☐ Review competitors' awards
- ☐ Establish award goals
- ☐ Research "top" magazine and newspaper lists
- ☐ Research using public relations specialists
- ☐ Review awards provided by associations
- ☐ Review awards provided by organizations
- ☐ Review awards provided by magazines
- ☐ Review awards provided by newspapers
- ☐ Research credentials of employees
- ☐ Review employees' vendor certifications
- ☐ Review employees' industry certifications
- ☐ Review employees' educational backgrounds
- ☐ Review employees' awards of excellence
- ☐ Market credentials inside the office
- ☐ Market credentials outside the office
- ☐ Gather company-wide experience stats
- ☐ Gather company-wide certification stats
- ☐ Market athletic and charitable distinctions
- ☐ Market employees' strengths
- ☐ Establish employee certification paths
- ☐ Establish employee recognition paths
- ☐ Prioritize the company's resume building

Growing Affiliations

- ☐ Review current association memberships
- ☐ Review historical association members
- ☐ Review current official affiliations
- ☐ Review historical official affiliations
- ☐ Review the cost of all current memberships
- ☐ Review the value of all current memberships
- ☐ Research other available associations
- ☐ Research other available strategic alliances
- ☐ Compare competitors' associations
- ☐ Compare competitors' strategic alliances
- ☐ Research Internet-based alliances
- ☐ Establish all company-wide expertise

Checklist

- [ ] Research touting expertise through the media
- [ ] Research touting expertise on the Internet
- [ ] Research touting expertise using television
- [ ] Research touting expertise using radio
- [ ] Research writing traditional news columns
- [ ] Research writing online columns
- [ ] Research online ad sharing
- [ ] Buy online ads
- [ ] Host online ads
- [ ] Create online marketing referrals
- [ ] Explore search engine optimization
- [ ] Use Google Analytics for web traffic sources
- [ ] Adjust marketing based on Google Analytics
- [ ] Use social online network sites
- [ ] Use business online network sites
- [ ] Master Internet alliance-building tools
- [ ] Maintain current, accurate online information
- [ ] Remove ineffective associations and alliances

Step 3: Maximizing Cash Flow

Keeping the Cash Flowing

- [ ] Recognize cash flow problems
- [ ] Recognize historical cash flow problems
- [ ] Determine weekly cash flow needs
- [ ] Determine monthly cash flow needs
- [ ] Determine yearly cash flow needs
- [ ] Determine business income flow
- [ ] Recognize credit availability problems
- [ ] Recognize collection problems
- [ ] Recognize the cost of lack of cash
- [ ] Plot low and high cash flow periods
- [ ] Research competitors' credit procedures
- [ ] Research competitors' collection procedures
- [ ] Develop prepaid retainer plans
- [ ] Create incentives for prepaid retainer plans
- [ ] Create a contract based service model

☐ Match staff levels with contracted customers
☐ Develop prepaid maintenance contracts
☐ Tightly manage employee work schedules
☐ Coordinate schedules with collections
☐ Coordinate schedules with impending sales
☐ Coordinate schedules with contract renewals
☐ Coordinate schedules with retainer payments
☐ Manage new client work around cash flow
☐ Manage large jobs around cash flow
☐ Manage normal work flow around cash flow
☐ Prioritize any vendor commission income
☐ Prioritize any referral-based income
☐ Prioritize any cross-selling based income
☐ Match all purchases around credit availability
☐ Match purchases around cash flow
☐ Match purchases around work schedules
☐ Review all Accounts Payable vendor terms
☐ Renegotiate all Accounts Payable vendor terms
☐ Engage senior management in AP process
☐ Choose vendors with favorable terms
☐ Use credit cards to extend terms without interest
☐ Research cash-flow friendly goods to sell
☐ Enhance sales with cash-flow friendly goods
☐ Order all goods "just in time" for usage
☐ Tightly manage returns to vendors
☐ Tightly manage returns from clients
☐ Tightly manage credits to clients
☐ Tightly manage credits from vendors
☐ Utilize and manage vendor co-op funds
☐ Explore all possible cash flow alternatives

Knowing Your Budget
☐ Create a budget of all expenses
☐ Compare budgeted costs to last year
☐ Compare historical expense budgets
☐ Assign a senior manager to the budget analysis

Checklist

- ☐ Prepare a budget of all expected sales
- ☐ Compare budgeted sales to last year
- ☐ Compare historical sales budgets
- ☐ Consider renewable contracts in the sales budget
- ☐ Consider all new markets in the sales budget
- ☐ Consider sales to probable new clients
- ☐ Consider sales to existing clients
- ☐ Include all commissions in the sales budget
- ☐ Include all referral fees in the sales budget
- ☐ Project growth in relevant sales categories
- ☐ Project a decrease in relevant sales categories
- ☐ Project all retainer plan sales
- ☐ Project all maintenance contract sales
- ☐ Project all recurring client billing
- ☐ Review necessity of all prior year expenses
- ☐ Review price point of all prior year expenses
- ☐ Review historical expense budgets
- ☐ Compare last year's budget to actual numbers
- ☐ Review discrepancies in last year's budget
- ☐ Establish all mandatory expenses
- ☐ Establish all sales-dependent expenses
- ☐ Establish all discretionary expenses
- ☐ Project all increases to prior year budget items
- ☐ Project all decreases to prior year budget items
- ☐ Remove any unnecessary expenses
- ☐ Include all presales expenses
- ☐ Include all credit-card expense
- ☐ Include all owner benefits
- ☐ Include all entertainment expense
- ☐ Include all gift and donation expense
- ☐ Include all possible employee bonuses
- ☐ Include all out-going referral fees
- ☐ Include all out-going commissions
- ☐ Balance your budget
- ☐ Maintain on-going budget versus actual reporting
- ☐ Work in a real-time reporting environment

☐ Tweak budgets continually for changes to sales
☐ Tweak budgets continually for changes to expenses

Working to the Bottom Line

☐ Learn the value of a Job Costing system
☐ Maintain an integrated Job Costing system
☐ Research historical Job Costing data
☐ Utilize budgets for Job Costing
☐ Measure budget versus actual Job Cost data
☐ Price sales to be profitable using Job Cost data
☐ Analyze Job Cost profit for each sale
☐ Analyze Job Cost profit by job type
☐ Analyze Job Cost profit by product content
☐ Analyze Job Cost profit by customer
☐ Analyze Job Cost profit by salesperson
☐ Analyze Job Cost profit by service provider
☐ Learn the value of a Time and Billing system
☐ Maintain an integrated Time and Billing system
☐ Research historical Time and Billing data
☐ Measure employee down and overhead time
☐ Measure net profit by job basis after labor costs
☐ Measure profit on a daily, monthly, yearly basis
☐ Learn the value of analyzing labor utilization
☐ Measure labor utilization by employee
☐ Measure labor utilization month to month
☐ Measure labor utilization year to year
☐ Determine pricing based on Time and Billing data
☐ Determine sales based on Time and Billing data
☐ Create deliverable objectives for employees

Step 4: Streamlining Management Costs

Changing the Back-Office Focus

☐ Review functions of the back office
☐ Remove administrative-heavy processes
☐ Create a sales-driving back office

Checklist

- ☐ Create a customer support back office
- ☐ Create a customer service back office
- ☐ Review all data entry methods
- ☐ Review all information management methods
- ☐ Review all system integration
- ☐ Reduce redundancy
- ☐ Increase redundant-removing training
- ☐ Establish a data entry sense of urgency
- ☐ Establish a data management sense of urgency
- ☐ Establish an administrative sense of urgency
- ☐ Establish a sense of urgency with financial data
- ☐ Manage a synchronized, real-time financial system
- ☐ Establish timely management of employee data
- ☐ Establish timely management of client data
- ☐ Establish timely management of vendor data
- ☐ Establish timely management of Job Cost data
- ☐ Establish timeliness of Time and Billing data
- ☐ Revisit budget changes continuously
- ☐ Maintain up-to-the-minute CRM data
- ☐ Create up-to-the-minute sales projections
- ☐ Manage a real-time Profit and Loss system
- ☐ Manage a real-time Cash Flow system
- ☐ Manage a time-sensitive Job Cost system
- ☐ Manage time-sensitive Time and Billing data
- ☐ Manage time-sensitive labor utilization data
- ☐ Establish timely business management reports
- ☐ Manage updated tech support information
- ☐ Manage updated training requirement data
- ☐ Manage updated vendor information
- ☐ Manage updated office procedure data
- ☐ Manage updated sales information
- ☐ Manage updated marketing data for employees
- ☐ Manage updated marketing data for clients
- ☐ Manage updated website data
- ☐ Manage client sales reporting month to month
- ☐ Manage client sales reporting year to year

- ☐ Manage client profit reporting
- ☐ Establish alerts when client spending changes
- ☐ Establish alerts when client pricing changes
- ☐ Establish timely open purchase order reports
- ☐ Establish timely client contract renewals
- ☐ Establish timely cash flow projections
- ☐ Establish timely customer lead reporting
- ☐ Create back-office control of all outsourcing
- ☐ Create approvals for outsourced enhancements
- ☐ Oversee outsourced software updating
- ☐ Oversee outsourced security monitoring
- ☐ Oversee outsourced backup reporting
- ☐ Oversee outsourced hardware maintenance
- ☐ Oversee outsourced email hosting
- ☐ Oversee outsourced website hosting
- ☐ Oversee outsourced Internet service
- ☐ Manage all outsourced performance
- ☐ Manage all Internet advertising spending
- ☐ Manage online recruiting spending
- ☐ Create in-house process management review
- ☐ Scan and file all company contracts
- ☐ Scan and file all company authorizations
- ☐ Create a double storage system for documents
- ☐ Establish tight computer system security
- ☐ Manage employee policies for equipment use
- ☐ Manage electronic reporting of equipment use
- ☐ Establish properly managed data policies
- ☐ Establish a networked information system
- ☐ Establish shared company-wide data
- ☐ Establish shared client data
- ☐ Establish shared vendor data
- ☐ Establish shared client proposals and contracts
- ☐ Establish shared client history and financials
- ☐ Establish shared vendor product and sales data
- ☐ Establish shared vendor history data
- ☐ Establish shared vendor tech support data
- ☐ Utilize the company website for data sharing

☐ Utilize shared contact, work and calendar data
☐ Support all company-wide systems

Managing for Profit

☐ Define all service provider employees
☐ Define all back-office employees
☐ Define back-office client service work
☐ Create back-office client service billables
☐ Create back-office client service Job Costs
☐ Define back-office client management work
☐ Create back-office client management billing
☐ Create back-office client management Job Costs
☐ Define service providers' managerial tasks
☐ Create managerial billing for service providers
☐ Create managerial billing in Job Cost data
☐ Manage all costs of goods in Job Cost data
☐ Research the components of client invoices
☐ Cover back-office client work in fixed prices
☐ Cover back-office management in fixed prices
☐ Cover service providers' management in sales
☐ Cover all costs of goods in fixed prices
☐ Utilize Time and Billing for all client labor
☐ Manage budgets versus actual fixed priced jobs
☐ Research increasing fixed prices to clients
☐ Research reducing labor in fixed priced jobs
☐ Research reducing deliverables in fixed prices
☐ Research a flat management fee bill on invoices
☐ Cover back-office services in hourly bills
☐ Cover managerial services in hourly bills
☐ Cover all costs of goods in hourly bills
☐ Research use of multi-tiered billing rates
☐ Create multitiered billing rates in hourly billing
☐ Create multitiered billing rates in Job Costing
☐ Research any lost profit centers in operation
☐ Create a more client-billable back office
☐ Create client-billed service provider management

Step 5: Raising the Marketing Bar

Networking

- ☐ Establish current networking venues
- ☐ Review historical networking venues
- ☐ Research face-to-face networking opportunities
- ☐ Research Internet networking opportunities
- ☐ Analyze cost-effectiveness of all networking
- ☐ Analyze time-effectiveness of all networking
- ☐ Review social online networking in use
- ☐ Review business online networking in use
- ☐ Review employee social online network profiles
- ☐ Review employee business online network profiles
- ☐ Review company social online network profiles
- ☐ Review company business online network profiles
- ☐ Explore seeking sales on online networks
- ☐ Explore marketing on online networks
- ☐ Explore recruiting on online networks
- ☐ Review company Wikipedia profiles
- ☐ Review employee Wikipedia profiles
- ☐ Explore competitors' networking avenues
- ☐ Explore competitors' online profiles
- ☐ Review business videos on YouTube
- ☐ Create business videos on YouTube
- ☐ Explore use of Twitter
- ☐ Utilize Twitter
- ☐ Research business blogs
- ☐ Create a company blog
- ☐ Update other pertinent blogs
- ☐ Establish Internet savvy current employees
- ☐ Utilize in-house talent to create blogs
- ☐ Utilize in-house talent to create news columns
- ☐ Research historical company news columns
- ☐ Research pertinent online news publications
- ☐ Contribute to online news columns
- ☐ Market using online publications
- ☐ Use publications for search engine optimization

- ☐ Use Google Analytics to judge publication traffic
- ☐ Check search engine results after publications
- ☐ Market your online presence to your customers
- ☐ Research web conferencing options
- ☐ Utilize web conferencing for clients
- ☐ Utilize web conferencing for employees
- ☐ Utilize web conference for sales prospects
- ☐ Analyze face-to-face versus web meetings
- ☐ Market periodic web sales conferences
- ☐ Create global or national web conference presence
- ☐ Utilize web conferencing for presentations
- ☐ Utilize web conferencing for meetings
- ☐ Utilize web conferencing for training
- ☐ Utilize web conferencing for support services
- ☐ Upgrade web presentation skills
- ☐ Research online forums in your market space
- ☐ Research business community forums
- ☐ Utilize in-house talent for forum management
- ☐ Research available news outlets
- ☐ Research vendor and private forums
- ☐ Research available webcasts
- ☐ Research webcast attendance by customers
- ☐ Research webcast attendance by competitors
- ☐ Utilize webcasts for marketing and sales
- ☐ Utilize webcasts for product presentations
- ☐ Utilize webcasts for service presentations
- ☐ Research available podcasts
- ☐ Invest in creating podcast lectures
- ☐ Invest in creating podcast training
- ☐ Invest in creating podcast marketing
- ☐ Utilize in-house talent for webcast production
- ☐ Utilize in-house talent for podcast production

Covering All Bases

- ☐ Create a marketing plan
- ☐ Review historical marketing plans
- ☐ Compare changes in previous marketing plans

Appendix B: Scheduling the Changes

- ☐ Measure word of mouth and reference referrals
- ☐ Create a marketing budget
- ☐ Review standard business presentations
- ☐ Update business cards
- ☐ Update letterhead and envelopes
- ☐ Update brochures
- ☐ Update website
- ☐ Register in online Internet registries
- ☐ Update online business profiles
- ☐ Research syndicated business and vendor material
- ☐ Utilize syndicated material on your website
- ☐ Establish online links to affiliates
- ☐ Compare marketing tools with competitors
- ☐ Research marketing by start-up businesses
- ☐ Research presentations by start-up businesses
- ☐ Research state-of-the-art marketing material
- ☐ Update marketing material with credentials
- ☐ Update marketing material with expertise
- ☐ Market YouTube, LinkedIn presence
- ☐ Market Twitter, Facebook presence
- ☐ Review all current advertising methods
- ☐ Research cost-effectiveness of all advertising
- ☐ Utilize vendor co-op funds for print ads
- ☐ Utilize vendor co-op funds for newsletters
- ☐ Utilize online advertising
- ☐ Monitor costs and results of online advertising
- ☐ Cross-link to complementary service providers
- ☐ Use keywords to gain search engine dominance
- ☐ Research cost-effectiveness of direct mail pieces
- ☐ Research cost-effectiveness of mailed newsletters
- ☐ Research mass email service providing companies
- ☐ Mass email newsletters and direct mail pieces
- ☐ Measure statistics of mass email exposure
- ☐ Utilize brand marketing
- ☐ Explore radio marketing opportunities
- ☐ Explore television marketing opportunities
- ☐ Outsource sophisticated marketing functions

Checklist

- ☐ Utilize outsourcing for article placement
- ☐ Utilize outsourcing for press releases
- ☐ Promote your good will and philanthropic efforts
- ☐ Teach classes
- ☐ Give speeches
- ☐ Serve as a professional reference
- ☐ Research referral sources
- ☐ Enhance vendor referral sources
- ☐ Formalize referral requests
- ☐ Explore private referral agencies
- ☐ Solicit client recommendations
- ☐ Market recommendations to clients and vendors
- ☐ Maintain face-to-face marketing programs
- ☐ Attend trade shows and conferences
- ☐ Present at trade shows and conferences
- ☐ Research virtual trade show services
- ☐ Host a virtual trade show
- ☐ Present face to face to customers
- ☐ Web conference one on one to customers
- ☐ Lecture at continuing education forums
- ☐ Present at local associations and bookstores
- ☐ Utilize telemarketers
- ☐ Engage salespeople in direct sales efforts
- ☐ Measure your presence in your marketplace

Strategizing
- ☐ Research previous marketing measuring tools
- ☐ Research ROI marketing analyses
- ☐ Identify satisfactory marketing programs
- ☐ Identify successful marketing programs
- ☐ Identify your current CRM process
- ☐ Learn the value of an integrated CRM system
- ☐ Create integration from CRM to Accounting
- ☐ Identify sales reporting requirements
- ☐ Create reports for sales projections
- ☐ Create reports for salesperson activity
- ☐ Create reports for client activity

☐ Create reports for client interests
☐ Equate all prior sales with marketing methods
☐ Equate all prior customers with lead source
☐ Enter all customers into a CRM system
☐ Enter all prospective clients into a CRM system
☐ Track the lead source of every new prospect
☐ Track marketing effort of every new sale
☐ Maintain data entry completeness and accuracy
☐ Establish stranger-contact measurement
☐ Utilize mass email statistics on readership
☐ Utilize mass newsletter readership statistics
☐ Attribute website access to marketing efforts
☐ Measure telemarketing activity
☐ Measure marketing results to your own prospects
☐ Develop subtle judgments of marketing campaigns
☐ Statistically compare marketing and sales efforts
☐ Revise marketing campaigns based on results

Step 6: Making Everyone a Salesperson

Enlisting the Troops
☐ Define an expense-oriented business model
☐ Define a sales-oriented business model
☐ Establish sales-oriented training sessions
☐ Establish office management
☐ Establish office process monitoring
☐ Establish telephone protocol
☐ Establish email protocol
☐ Promote a positive attitude in the office
☐ Promote professionalism in the office
☐ Utilize emails as marketing tools
☐ Utilize signatures and reference links in emails
☐ Promote a professional dress code
☐ Maintain professional Internet profiles
☐ Maintain professional cell phone and texting use
☐ Establish policy surrounding office system use
☐ Promote company material as proprietary

- ☐ Establish security procedures
- ☐ Promote company-enhancing contributions
- ☐ Enlist out-of-role marketing assistance
- ☐ Promote sales and marketing opportunities
- ☐ Research sales opportunities while recruiting
- ☐ Perform market research on competitors
- ☐ Perform market research on potential sales
- ☐ Foster new employee ideas
- ☐ Create a standard of excellence
- ☐ Provide opportunities for employee growth
- ☐ Provide advancement through publications
- ☐ Provide advancement through certifications
- ☐ Provide advancement through idea generation
- ☐ Explore changes to office culture
- ☐ Promote the sales-oriented culture
- ☐ Explore successful office patterns
- ☐ Explore change

Creating a Mantra

- ☐ Investigate the overall office attitude
- ☐ Seek problem-solving employees
- ☐ Seek profit-geared employees
- ☐ Promote client service oriented recommendations
- ☐ Seek advice from back-office management
- ☐ Seek office generated procedural recommendations
- ☐ Explore what is successful with clients
- ☐ Explore what is successful with employees
- ☐ Explore satisfaction with products
- ☐ Explore satisfaction with services
- ☐ Explore dissatisfaction with products
- ☐ Explore dissatisfaction with services
- ☐ Establish whether clients are generally happy
- ☐ Establish if employees are generally happy
- ☐ Explore competing solutions
- ☐ Research client approval rating of employees
- ☐ Research employee peer approval ratings
- ☐ Explore company spending patterns

☐ Establish employees needing management
☐ Establish employees providing management
☐ Create company watchdogs
☐ Promote entrepreneurial behavior
☐ Promote client pleasing behavior
☐ Promote sales enhancing behavior
☐ Promote profit generating behavior
☐ Market the company from within

Worksheets

Time Requirements:

Step	Quarter	Total Time Required

Employee Scheduling:

Employee	Available Time Per Quarter

Priority Scheduling:		
Quarter	Time Required	Employee Time Available

Reevaluating Each Area Over and Over Again in the Future

Congratulations! You have spent the time to decide what changes should be made in your business model.

You have looked at your sales model, your expense spending, and your administrative operation. You have taken a hard look at your image and your connections to the outside world. You have looked at cash flow in a way that is painful but filled with a promise for less stress in the future. You have committed to put a greater emphasis on your budget and decided that losses are something to avoid, not foster. Maintaining a completely sales-driven, profit-oriented organization will replace the daily preoccupation with meeting payroll and balancing the checkbook. Marketing is back where it should be on the tip of your tongue and every employee is now thinking income versus expense.

So, this invigorating feeling, this challenge, and this hope for the future—how can we guarantee that it will not end? Can we know that all of these efforts will solve the problems that we had faced in the past? Certainly, the adrenalin burst that enabled such an undertaking won't go on forever. What can be done to avoid returning to old habits and, thus, old losses?

185

Well, it isn't easy and competition is still everywhere.

So, just as there were new business models to explore, more modern tools of the trade to employ, and some housecleaning efforts that were long past due, a constant reevaluation strategy needs to be part of the workday.

All of the hard work that has been performed won't stay in place unless there is a solid maintenance plan in place. There is measuring, analyzing, strategizing, and reinventing. Processes are fluid and change is inevitable. So, there is one last lesson to learn and that is to reevaluate—thoroughly and often.

Just as a checkbook needs to have on-going reconciliation, the success and failure of every aspect of your business model needs on-going review. If you have brought profit back into your limelight, make sure that you keep it there.

About the Author

Patricia Sigmon is the CEO of LPS Consulting Co., Inc., a computer consulting firm serving the metropolitan New York area. Founded by Patricia in 1983, LPS is a first-generation PC systems integration firm, specializing in full-service hardware and software implementation for small to mid-size businesses. As the computer industry has evolved, LPS has changed from a software development firm into a reseller of the most prominent software solutions on the market.

Patricia has served as a speaker, lecturer, and advisor for start-up and fellow business owners throughout the United States. She is also the founder and president of David Advisory Group, whose mission is to provide advice to CEOs and presidents of privately-held, small to midsize service-based businesses in the areas of practice management and profit generation.

Patricia has a degree in computer science from Rutgers University and currently splits her residence between Central New Jersey and New York City.

She can be reached at psigmon@davidadvisorygroup.com.

Index

Index

Index